learn
to use
power.
point
2000

THIS IS A SEVENOAKS BOOK

Text and design copyright © Carlton Books 2000

A CIP Catalogue for this book is available from the British Library

ISBN 1 86200 071 9

Project Editor: Lara Maiklem
Production: Sarah Corteel

Created by Gecko Grafx Ltd

Notice of Liability
Every effort has been made to ensure that this book contains accurate and current information. However, the Publisher and the author shall not be liable for any loss or damage suffered by the readers as a result of any information contained herein.

Trademarks
Microsoft® PowerPoint 2000®, Office 2000® and Windows® are registered trademarks of Microsoft Corporation.
All other trademarks are acknowledged as belonging to their respective companies.

Printed and bound in Italy.

learn to use
power.point 2000

Christophe Dillinger

SEVENOAKS

CONTENTS

GETTING STARTED

1

Microsoft PowerPoint is the world's most popular presentation program. A key part of office life, it allows users to prepare slideshows, informative displays, presentations and important strategic documents quickly and easily. PowerPoint 2000 is as clear and intuitive as its earlier cousins. In this section, we'll look at the basics of installing and using the program – how to set PowerPoint up, run it, start new documents and manage your files.

INSTALLING POWERPOINT

Installing PowerPoint 2000 is as simple as putting the CD into the drive and answering a few questions. You will be shown a screen asking you some personal details, including your full name, your initials (for marking revisions and such-like) and the CD key, the product's serial number. Enter all this in and click on Next. The CD key is not case-sensitive, which means that you can type it in lower or upper case.

Your user details only need to be entered once when setting up PowerPoint 2000.

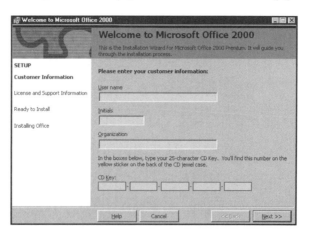

WHAT YOU NEED

The Standard version of the Microsoft Office requires a Pentium 75mhz computer or better, and Windows 95 or later. It can also run on an NT Workstation running Version 3, System Pack 4 or later. You'll need to have at least 16 MB of Ram (32 for NT) and 189 MB of free disk space on your hard drive. You'll also need a CD-ROM drive, and a VGA or better monitor.

INSTALL NOW

Once you've entered a valid CD key serial number, you will progress to Microsoft's standard user license. You have to accept this in order to install the program, so do so. Next, you'll see the Installation screen. Unless you specifically want to make some alterations to Microsoft's recommended installation – for instance to avoid installing Outlook, the Office Email program – tell the install program to proceed with a standard set-up by clicking on <u>Install Now</u>. This will install PowerPoint, along with the various shared tools it needs to function properly, and the other Microsoft Office programs included with it, such as Microsoft Word. You will be shown the details, and asked if you want to proceed. Click <u>OK</u>. Microsoft Office will be installed on your computer. This may take several minutes, and the installation program will need to restart your computer before it can finish off. Once it has done everything and returned you to Windows, you are ready to run PowerPoint.

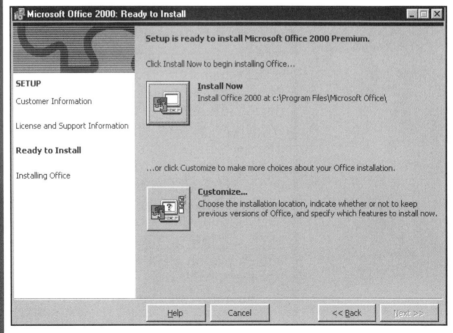

With the Ready to Install screen, you can click on <u>Install Now</u> to start the installation process or you can <u>Customize...</u> your installation.

Choose what you
want to install and
where you want to
install it.

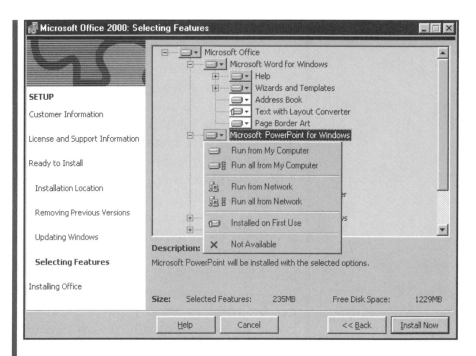

CUSTOM INSTALLATION

There are two things to consider when doing a custom install
of Microsoft Office. One is to choose a location on your hard
drive for the programs to be installed into, and the other is to
select which Office components are going to be included.
Selecting a location is relatively simple. You can either accept
the default option of installing the Office into the newly-
created Microsoft Office subdirectory of the C:/Program Files/
directory, or you can select a new location. The default option
will be fine for almost everyone. Choosing which parts of the
Office to install – known as Selecting Features – is quite a lot
more complicated, as the picture here shows.

The contents of Microsoft Office are displayed in the
Microsoft Office 2000: Selecting Features dialog. At first, this
will show you a list of the main components of the Office –
PowerPoint, Word, Excel, Outlook and so on – that come with
the version you have purchased. The programs are shown as
a file map, with a + sign before them to indicate that some
subcomponents of that program are still hidden. You can click
on the + to reveal the next layer of extra tools and optional

items associated with that program. For example, <u>Microsoft PowerPoint</u> for Windows hides the Help subcomponents, which in turn hides the Office Assistant subcomponents, and so on. Clicking on the dropdown box just to the left of each program lets you choose to install it <u>(Run From My Computer)</u>, install it and all its subcomponents <u>(Run All From My Computer)</u>, install it when you first start it <u>(Installed on First Use)</u>, or not install it at all <u>(Not Available)</u>. The icon for that program will change as appropriate. If the icon is white, that program and all its subcomponents are due to be installed either immediately or on first use. If there is no ± for the item, it has no sub-components. If you want a full installation of PowerPoint, click on it and select <u>Run All From My Computer</u>. So long as the <u>Selected Features</u> total is less than the <u>Free Disk Space</u> total, the installation will fit on your hard drive. When you have selected the various components you want, click on the <u>Install Now</u> button and your custom installation will be performed. You can add or remove bits later by running the Office 2000 CD again, so it doesn't matter too much if you miss something, or install more than you wanted.

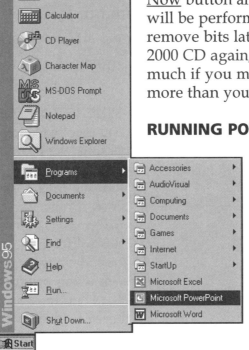

RUNNING POWERPOINT

The installation process will place icons for your new Microsoft Office programs into your Programs folder for you automatically. These are shown above, and provide a handy short-cut for starting PowerPoint or any other component of Microsoft Office.

FILE MANAGEMENT

Having a well-thought-out set of folders for your documents will make your life a lot easier once you've been using PowerPoint for a while. If you put everything in the same folder without thinking too much about what you're calling your documents, the time will come when you're faced with a long list of obscurely-titled files, and it will be difficult and time-consuming to work out which one you want each time, and even more unpleasant trying to sort them out. Preparing a good structure for your folders will repay you several times over in the long run.

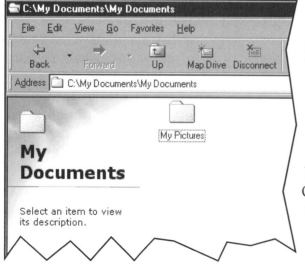

WHERE TO STORE DOCUMENTS

The best place to start your own personal set of document folders is inside the folder titled My Documents, which you will find is already on your desktop. PowerPoint, like other Microsoft Office programs, is already set to work with this folder, so it makes the best choice for a starting-point. If you've been using programs from Microsoft Office before, you may well find that there are already Office documents inside My Documents. That isn't going to be a problem.

1 Double-click on the <u>My Documents</u> icon on your desktop and it will open up. Then place the mouse pointer inside the folder contents display area and right-click. A pick-list menu of options will open up next to your pointer. Hold the pointer over the selection <u>New</u>, and a new documents sub-menu will appear. The top option is <u>Folder</u>; click on that.

CREATING YOUR OWN FOLDERS

Setting up your own folders inside <u>My Documents</u> is easy.

2 A new folder will appear next to the mouse pointer, called <u>New Folder</u>. Anything you type now, before you press the mouse again, will become the folder's new name. We suggest you call this folder PowerPoint.

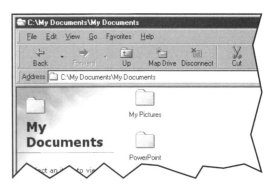

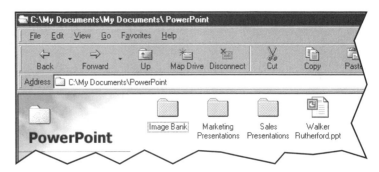

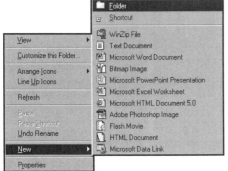

3 Double-click on the new PowerPoint folder to open it. You can now follow the process in 1 and 2 above to create a new folder for each different category of document you will be creating with Microsoft PowerPoint 2000. These can be folders named after departments or clients you deal with, or different types of function – presentations, notices, slideshows and so on – or even just as simple a division as calling folders Personal and Business.

SENSIBLE STORAGE　　　　　　　　　　　　_ 🗗 ✕

You can also add further folders inside any folder you create here – so Business could have subfolders for Incoming and Outgoing. You could of course store documents inside your PowerPoint folder too, if they don't fit any of the categories you've created.

OPENING A DOCUMENT

There are two ways to open a PowerPoint document. If you are in Windows but PowerPoint is not running, the quickest way to open a document is to double-click on it. This will start Microsoft PowerPoint up automatically, load your document into PowerPoint and present it ready for you to start working on it. All you have to do is find where the document is stored – within the sub-folder PowerPoint inside the desktop folder My Documents, if you have set up a file structure as we recommend – and double-click its icon.

Find your PowerPoint documents and double-click on them to start the program.

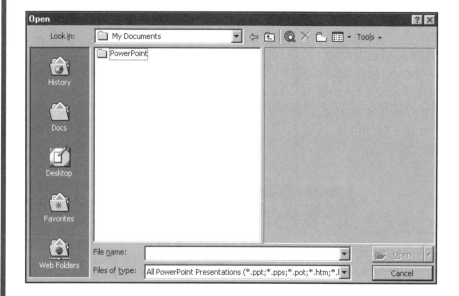

If you do have PowerPoint already running, you can open a file by selecting the Open command from the FILE menu, or clicking on the folder-like Open File icon on the main toolbar. This will give you the Open dialog box, which shows you the contents of your My Documents folder by default. You can then double-click on the PowerPoint folder within the box to enter it, continue through your folder structure to the file you want and then double-click on it to load it into PowerPoint. You can also use the Back Up icon to move one step backwards inside your folders, showing you the folder that holds the one you are currently looking at.

SAVING AND CLOSING

It's important to make sure that you don't lose your work. When you've finished with one presentation for the time being, save it by selecting Save from the FILE menu or clicking on the Disk icon on the main toolbar. If the workbook is one you have newly created, you will need to give it a name and tell the computer where to store it. You will see a dialog box called Save As, similar to the Open dialog.

Move through to the folder you want to save it in by navigating as before, type the name you want the document to be called in the box File Name and click Save. Try to make sure that the document name explains the contents – "March 12 Sales Presentation", for example.

Knowing where to open your files from and where to save them to is vital.

POWERPOINT DOCUMENTS

When you create a document in PowerPoint, it is referred to as a **Presentation**. The files that PowerPoint uses are described in Windows Explorer as being either of type Microsoft PowerPoint Presentation (with a **.ppt** file extension) or Microsoft PowerPoint Template (with a **.pot** file extension).

STARTING A DOCUMENT

Being able to start PowerPoint by double-clicking on a document is all well and good, but it won't be much use to you until you have some presentations of your own. Over the next few pages, we'll look at how to start up a new document.

PRESENTATIONS

Before we discuss actually creating a new presentation, though, it's worth taking a moment to consider what you would generally use PowerPoint for. If you want to work with a lot of text, you're better off with Word, and if you need to

manipulate data, you're better off with Excel. If, however, you need to mix text and graphics in an easy, eye-catching way, then PowerPoint is by far the best tool for the job. PowerPoint Presentations are typically printed on to slides or overhead transparency sheets (for use during, well, presentations), turned into brochures or pitch documents or used to provide on-screen illustrations and informative slide shows.

THE <u>POWERPOINT</u> DIALOG

When you start PowerPoint – assuming that you have not double-clicked on an existing presentation – the program shows you a dialog box called <u>PowerPoint</u>, from which you can choose any of the various options for starting a new document. The top half of the dialog is a box entitled <u>Create a new presentation using</u>, which allows you to click on a button for the <u>AutoContent Wizard</u>, a <u>Design Template</u> or a <u>Blank Presentation</u>. The AutoContent Wizard is an extremely easy and powerful way of preparing a presentation more or less from scratch, and we'll discuss it in more detail over the page. A Design Template is a set of graphical styles and pre-sets for type fonts, button images, slide backgrounds and so on that will give your presentation a slick, consistent appearance. A Blank Presentation, finally, is just that. In the lower half of the dialog, you can also choose to open an existing presentation – <u>More Files</u> gives you the normal <u>Open</u> dialog. Make your choice, and click <u>OK</u>.

CUT THE DIALOG

You can tell PowerPoint not to show the opening dialog. If you do, you can get to the AutoContent Wizard by clicking <u>New</u> from the <u>FILE</u> menu, then selecting the <u>General</u> tab and double-clicking the <u>AutoContent Wizard</u> selection.

THE AUTOCONTENT WIZARD

By far the quickest and easiest way of creating an effective, balanced presentation that you can rely on to be properly paced and comprehensive is with the aid of the AutoContent Wizard. Its various templates have been prepared by expert speakers and management consultants, and each one is at least as professional and efficient as the information you could get from an instructional book.

1 When you start the Wizard, you'll see a welcome page in the middle of the screen entitled <u>AutoContent Wizard</u>. Click <u>Next</u> to get to the first stage, selecting a template. Click on a button from the column of categories. When you click a button, the templates available in that category will be shown to you. Select one, and click <u>Next</u>. If you're having trouble deciding, the templates are described towards the end of the book.

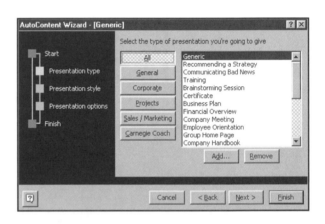

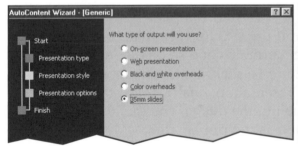

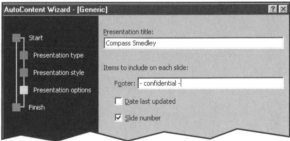

2 Next, you need to select the end purpose of your presentation, from an on-screen display to 35mm slides. PowerPoint uses this information to set your presentation slides to the correct size and colour gradings. Click on the button next to your required option, and click <u>Next</u>.

3 Finally, you need to tell PowerPoint the title of your presentation, and specify what you want to appear at the bottom of each slide. As well as the slide number (which appears bottom left) and the last save date (which appears bottom right), you can add a piece of text to be displayed bottom centre on each slide. When you are ready, click <u>Finish</u>. (Clicking <u>Next</u> takes you to a screen advising you to click <u>Finish</u>, which can be bypassed.)

USING AUTOCONTENT WIZARD OUTPUT

Although the AutoContent Wizard claims that your presentation is complete once it has generated it, that is not strictly true. It produces the appropriate slides, in the correct order, for a presentation of that type. The slides are laid out attractively in a complementary style, with the various categories and headings required listed. All you have to do is go through the presentation, slide by slide, and type in your information to replace the guide comments that the Wizard is pre-set for… but that is actually quite a lot of work. When you are working with the slides, it is usually best to resist the temptation to add information, tinker with the layout or change design elements. Just replace the generic text on each slide with appropriate text for your own presentation.

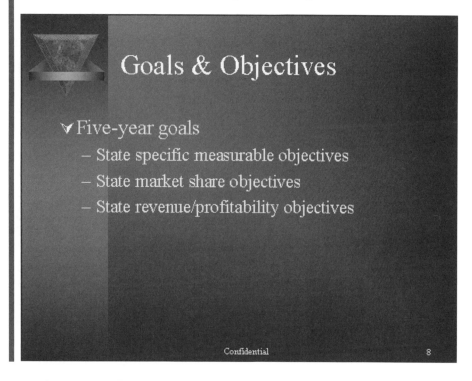

As you can see here, some of the dummy text on the AutoContent Wizard slides is very easy to replace – as in the slide title – while other bits are quite a lot more complicated to work with, such as the financial data area. Despite this, the AutoContent Wizard is still by far the best way to get started with PowerPoint and build up confidence.

THE GOLDEN RULES

There are three major things that you should do your best to keep in mind at all times when working with PowerPoint. They are simple, but they will go a long way to making sure that everything goes smoothly. Without them, you will find yourself becoming vulnerable to lost data and extreme frustration. Few things are as depressing as spending hours working on a presentation only to lose all your hard work through a simple slip.

The ever-popular (and often essential) Undo and Redo buttons. These options are also available from the File menu (see next page).

RULE ONE: UNDO MISTAKES

When you have made a mistake, the first place to look for help is the Undo function. You can access it by selecting Undo at the top of the Edit menu, by clicking on the Undo icon on the main toolbar, or by holding Ctrl down and pressing Z (Ctrl-Z). Undo works because PowerPoint stores a record of everything you do to your presentation, in the order you do it in. Then, if you want to undo something you have done – even after a short period of time – you can select Undo, item by item, until the mistake has been corrected. If you over-write some information you needed (or even erase the data in your entire presentation by accident, which is very difficult), just Undo the mistake and it will be as if you had never made the mistake in the first place. If you then change your mind and want to redo it, the Redo command is situated next to the Undo command on the toolbar and menu.

The most important thing to remember about <u>Undo</u> – apart from the fact that it is there for you – is that it only works on mistakes made since you last loaded the document. If you make a serious mistake do not, under any circumstances, save the flawed document over the older, previously correct document. Don't close or save the wrong document until you've tried to correct things with <u>Undo</u>, and if you do save it, use a new name so that you at least have the earlier versions to fall back on.

The <u>Save</u> icon, as it appears on menu bars.

RULE TWO: SAVE OFTEN

The best way of protecting yourself against mistakes and computer crashes is to save the documents that you are working on regularly. PowerPoint will automatically save recovery files for you in case the machine crashes, and it can be told to create a backup of the last version of the file for you automatically, but neither of these protections is quite as safe as making sure that you save your file regularly. If you are busy with a lengthy presentation, it is worth pausing every 15 minutes to check that your work is correct and then, once you're happy that it is right, saving the document. There is no substitute for saving your work. If you make a point of saving your presentation every 15 minutes then, even in the most serious cases, the worst that can happen to you is that you lose the last 15 minutes of work.

In addition to selecting <u>Save</u> from the <u>File</u> menu, you can also access it in two slightly quicker ways. One is to click on the small disk icon near the left-hand side of the main toolbar, and the other is to press <u>Control+S</u> on the keyboard. Both of those will perform a so-called Background Save, storing your data quickly without holding up the entire computer, so you can continue working.

RULE THREE: BACK UP YOUR DATA

Being secure about protecting your work also involves making extra copies on floppy disks, Zip disks or even CDs. At the end of every day, you should ideally make a copy of your work on an external drive or other removable storage device of some sort, which you should keep in a different location to your computer – at home, in the office safe, in someone else's office – anywhere away from your hard disk. This may seem over the top, and will often be vaguely inconvenient, but the fact remains that thieves usually take all available floppy disks, Zips and CDs when they steal a computer system, and a fire is equally indiscriminate. If your documents and data would be difficult, time-consuming or expensive to replace, then you want to make absolutely sure you're not going to lose them if the worst happens. There's a saying that goes: "You don't know the value of what you have until you've lost it". You don't really want to find out the true value of your documents the hard way, do you?

Never forget to save your valuable work. This menu also shows your recent files list at the bottom.

INTRODUCING SLIDES

Slides are the building blocks of a PowerPoint presentation. Each one is, in effect, a separate, self-contained page of your document. Unlike the pages in a word processing document, however, the slides themselves are the most basic component of your work, rather that the words they contain. In this chapter, we'll look at slides more closely – what they are, and how to make the most of them.

2

WORKING WITH SLIDES

Unlike the familiar blank slates of most new Windows documents, most PowerPoint slides start off ready to accept certain types of data, such as a title, bulleted list, graph, picture or chart. There are 24 different pre-set slide AutoLayouts, and you must choose one of them when you create a new slide – although one is completely blank. We'll look at them more closely in a few pages.

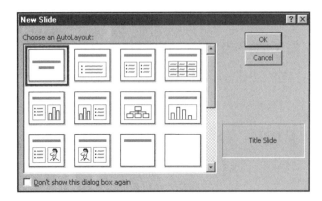

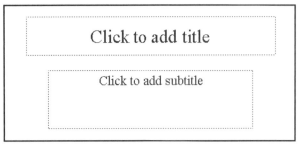

DIFFERENT SLIDE STYLES

When you start a new slide, it comes into existence containing a carefully-positioned box, called a <u>Placeholder</u>, for each data element that was on the slide layout you selected. Every layout apart from the blank slide contains a title; other options you can choose from include bulleted lists, organisation charts, data charts, subtitles, clip art, program objects and tables. Placeholders are never printed or shown in a slide show, and tell you what type of data they represent and what to do to activate it. They can be moved, resized or deleted, and you can add any of the elements by hand. We'll look at that later.

SLIDE SIZES

In addition to the different slide layouts that are available, you can also choose between a number of different slide sizes, depending on the end purpose you have for your presentation. You can't have slides of different sizes within the same presentation file, though, so you'll have to pick one size per file and stay with it. The default slide size is set for on-screen presentation, but that's easy to change.

2 The Page Setup dialog box will appear. In the top left, you will see a drop-down pick-list entitled Slides sized for:. Click on this to get a list of the preset sizes available. Click on one to apply its sizes.

1 From the FILE menu, select Page Setup.

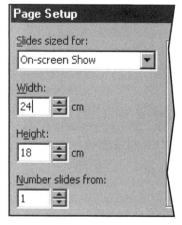

3 Alternatively, you can enter a custom page size manually by clicking and typing in the Height and Width boxes, and by choosing your page orientation for your main slides and for your speaker's notes in the Slides and Notes, Handouts & Outline areas respectively.

When you have entered the required details, click OK and your presentation will be automatically resized. Any preset design elements – such as slide backgrounds or bars – will also be fitted to the new size.

SLIDE HANDLING

Slides are extremely versatile, and PowerPoint provides several tools for manipulating them. We'll look at each of them in greater detail at various points later in the book, but for the moment it's worth just taking a moment to consider the various ways that you can work with your slides. One of the most important points to consider is the material that PowerPoint shows in the <u>Slide Outline</u> window to the left of the main slide display in <u>Normal View</u>. The text from headings, sub-headings and bullet lists is displayed here, slide by slide, using a system of indents that displays an item's relative importance. However, only items that were created by the <u>Slide Layout</u> will be displayed in this outline. If you create a text box, you cannot tell PowerPoint to treat it as a heading or other outline item.

However, the outline material can be manipulated, in some sense, as if it were one continuous document, with slides working more like section breaks. Individual outline items can be dragged and dropped within the outline, edited from inside it by clicking on them, or even promoted into new slides. Similarly, a slide title can be demoted to just a list item, erasing that slide. Graphical information, text boxes and layout on that slide will be lost, but the information stored in the outline will be appended to the previous slide. We'll go into promoting and demoting later on. For the moment, it is just important to know that although each slide is self-contained, the slide outlines are also treated as a form of continuous document.

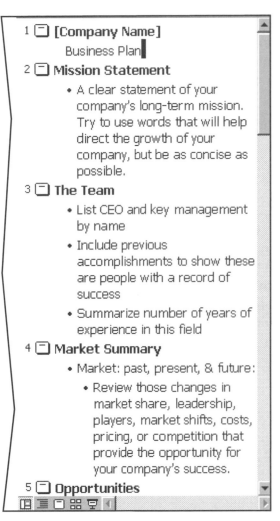

The <u>Slide Outline</u> window.

USING SLIDES SUCCESSFULLY

The secret of using slides successfully is working out exactly what you want to say, and saying it succinctly. PowerPoint documents are not really designed to give you the sort of space on a slide that will let you go into lengthy details, interesting asides and sub-points, extended justifications, and so on. They're really keyed towards short, punchy lists of items – which is why all the default text boxes on the slide layout are shown as bullet lists. The program originated as a way of providing support for people giving a speech, and when you make a presentation to a group of people, you do not want your visual aids to copy what you are saying word for word; you want them to summarize your key points clearly and succinctly. It is often quite difficult to get out of the habit of thinking of a computer document in terms of natural language – email and word processors encourage fully-written text. PowerPoint slides are more like newspaper headlines. Don't try to cram too much on to one slide. Leave plenty of space. Thinking in terms of lists and headlines – what computer people would call *Modular Structure* – will have great effects.

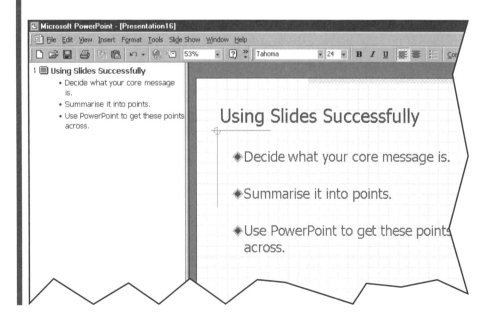

An example showing the <u>Slide Outline</u> window and its corresponding slide to the right.

THE AUTOCONTENT WIZARD

Earlier in this book, we mentioned the AutoContent Wizard, and how to use it. We're not going to go back over that basic information here, so if you're looking for instructions on operating it, see page 13. Instead, in this section we'll take a closer look at the Wizard, and examine some of the implications of its use. First-off, though, we'll have a quick look at the different types of presentation that the Wizard can produce for you.

PRESENTATION TYPES

The AutoContent Wizard has an impressive range of pre-formatted, content-organised documents available for your use. We'll look in detail at the individual templates towards the end of the book, so here we're just going to give you an overview of the different options available to you. Their names are all fairly self-explanatory, and should give you a solid idea of what the template contains.

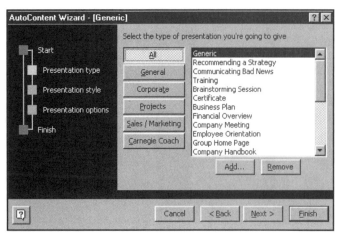

Choose from the impressive selection of AutoContent Wizard templates on offer.

CORPORATE PRESENTATIONS

The Corporate presentations relate primarily to business and management, and the most common tasks involved in preparing company-wide communications and related material. The **Business Plan** template is a cutting-edge presentation for structuring the information you're going to need when looking for finance to start up a company. It can also be adapted, with a little thought, to support a major project application. The **Financial Overview** is a structured template for presenting figures relating to company performance to the rest of the world, such as income, outgoings, share prices and regional data. It includes several charts, and is light on text.

The **Company Meeting** template is a detailed annual presentation on the state of the company, including a review of the previous year and the annual financial performance, a look at the company's current state and goals for the year to come. The **Employee Orientation** represents the information that a new company member needs to know – company history and policy, principal members, benefits, paperwork and so on. The **Group Home Page** template is a short corporate home page that would suit a small company, a department or a focused project team. Finally in the Corporate section, the **Company Handbook** is set up to provide contact details for the key personnel who are the first contact points for the assorted corporate and personnel functions, from accounts to personnel and training.

Balance Sheet

	1999	2000
Assets		
−Cash and short-term investments	$x,xxx	$x,xxx
−Accounts receivable	xxx	xxx
−Inventories	xxx	xxx
−Other	xxx	xxx
Total Assets	$x,xxx	$x,xxx
Liabilities		
−Accounts payable	$x,xxx	$x,xxx
−Accrued compensation	xxx	xxx
−Income taxes payable	xxx	xxx
−Other	xxx	xxx
Total Liabilities	$x,xxx	$x,xxx
Shareholder's Equity	$x,xxx	$x,xxx

Two examples of AutoContent Wizard templates: Financial Overview (above) and Group Home Page (below).

PROJECTS PRESENTATIONS

The Projects section of the AutoContent Wizard provides tools for the three stages of a project's life-span, from inception to completion. The **Project Overview** template allows you to define a project fully, detailing its scope, strategies and planning as well as other important issues. **Reporting Progress or Status** allows you to do just that – provide a briefing on how a project is performing, where its performance and scheduling matches expectations and where there is variance. Finally, the **Project Post-Mortem** allows for a detailed analysis of the project, its execution and realisation, providing scope for comparing performance with a range of different expectations.

The project Post-Mortem presentation with both the <u>Slide Outline</u> and <u>Slide</u> windows visible.

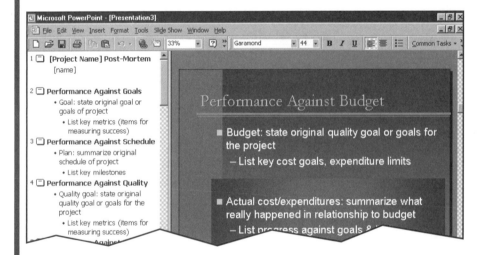

SALES & MARKETING PRESENTATIONS

This category covers presentations linked to the commercial exploitation of a product. Both **Selling a Product or Service** and **Product/Services Overview** are sales-led presentations, providing you with a framework for pitching a product. The former is a more aggressive presentation with effective closure, while the latter is more passive, looking primarily to inform. The **Marketing Plan** is an internal presentation, allowing you to discuss how a product or service is going to be marketed, what strategies and budgets are going to be needed.

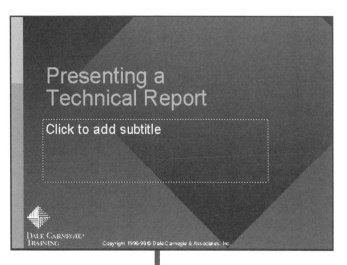

CARNEGIE COACH PRESENTATIONS

The presentations in the Carnegie Coach category have been specially designed for Microsoft by Dale Carnegie & Associates, Inc based on their famous training courses. Each one includes the structure that you will need, supplemented by clear instructional notes produced by the company. You will discover them to be invaluable if you find yourself in unfamiliar territory for a presentation. The presentations included with PowerPoint are **Selling Your Ideas**, **Motivating A Team**, **Facilitating A Meeting**, **Presenting A Technical Report**, **Managing Organizational Change** and **Introducing And Thanking A Speaker**.

GENERAL PRESENTATIONS

Finally, the general presentations are those that do not specifically fit in with any of the other categories. **Recommending a Strategy**, **Communicating Bad News** and **Brainstorming Session** all provide you with the basis for the meetings that their names would suggest. **Training** includes the structure for actually conducting a training or information session. **Certificate** is not a presentation at all, but is actually a one-page slide of a certificate that can be filled in and printed out as you need. Finally, **Generic** gives you the structure of a solid meeting with no specific content built in, so that no matter what the occasion you can tailor it to your needs.

AUTOCONTENT WIZARD OUTPUT

The real work involved in using the AutoContent Wizard comes after the presentation has been created. The templates that it creates are like frameworks, providing effective, ready-made structures for you to hang your presentation on rather than the completed work that the Wizard implies it will produce. You have to go through and replace the various placeholding points with real text and data. Given that fact, you may wonder why it is worth bothering with the Wizard at all, but in fact this approach is a strength rather than a weakness. The real value of the Wizard is in the structure of the document you are creating. There is far more to creating an effective piece of work than just getting the contents written. It would be disastrous to write a novel without

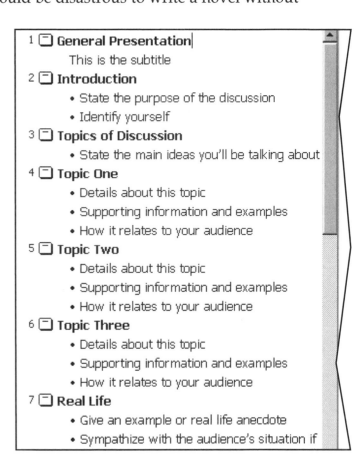

Use the <u>Slide Outline</u> view to get a clear overview of the whole presentation.

having some idea of how to go about preparing plot, characters, narrative and so on, and similarly there are rules and guidelines that are vital to the art of giving a presentation. You have to win your audience's attention and interest, present information in a manner they can understand, and structure your presentation to get your point across. In a book like this, there is no room to go into detail on the way you format and structure a successful presentation, but you have it all at your fingertips anyway – pre-prepared for you in the frameworks programmed into the AutoContent Wizard.

PERSONALIZATION

When the time comes to adapt the AutoContent Wizard presentation that you have chosen for your own needs, you need to remember to be flexible enough to break the rules when you need to, but cautious enough not to upset the balance. Let me explain. As the Wizard's templates are all general, so as to maximise their usefulness, you will occasionally come across areas of the presentation that are simply not relevant to your case. Don't be afraid to replace a slide's contents with something similar, or to add slides if you need to be more specific. Say, for example, that one of the Marketing presentations allocates a slide to look at the competition. You may simply not have any competition, because your product is internal, or unique. Alternatively, you may have three significant, well-known competitors, each of which is different enough to require slightly different discussion. In either case, the Wizard's default presentation should be modified. Don't make changes for the sake of it, though!

MODIFYING A PRESENTATION

Every element of the AutoContent Wizard's output can be modified to suit your needs, from the master slides and design templates through to the actual position of an item on the page. We'll go into the different ways you can modify slides in detail across the rest of the book, so for the moment just bear in mind that there is no element of an AutoContent presentation that cannot be changed if you see fit.

STARTING OPTIONS

If you choose not to use the AutoContent Wizard – and much of the time it will not be quite what you need – you still have several options to get you started. Over the next few pages, we'll take a look at design templates, slide layouts and getting started from a genuinely blank slate.

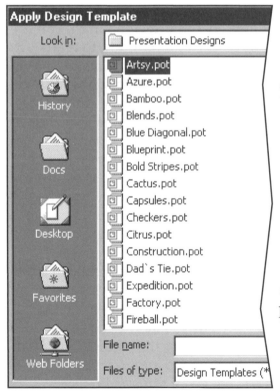

WHAT ARE DESIGN TEMPLATES?

A design template is a set of graphical elements and text styles that allow you to customise your presentation with a fully pre-designed look and feel. They provide a background image for the slides, complete with a complementary title slide, and include selections for your fonts, text sizes and colours, text box positions, header and footer details, chart and object styles and in fact everything else that can affect the look and feel of the final slides. Most of these options are set via the Master slides, which are used to provide a backdrop for all the slides you create. We will look at Master slides later. The templates have all been professionally designed and carefully balanced so that all the different elements work well together. Unlike the presentations in the AutoContent Wizard, Design Templates do not hold any text.

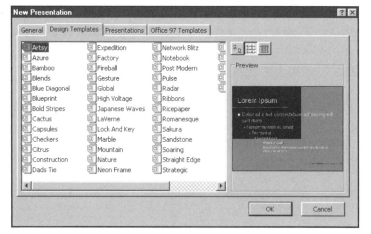

WHAT DESIGN TEMPLATES ARE AVAILABLE?

PowerPoint 2000 comes with 44 different design templates available for you to choose from, and you may be able to access more if you had previously installed older versions of the program. Unfortunately, we do not have the space here to show you an example of each one, but the Design Templates tab of the New Presentation dialog box – accessed by selecting New from the FILE menu or by selecting Design Template from the opening PowerPoint dialog – will let you quickly explore the options, showing you a preview of each as you highlight it.

You have quite a range available to you, from whimsical designs like **Dad's Tie** and **Strategic** through more classic layouts like **Marble** and **Romanesque** to business-like options such as **Blends** and **Global** and artistic sets such as **Ricepaper** and **Whirlpool**.

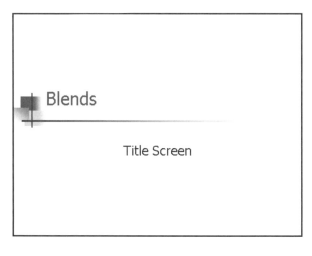

BLANK DOCUMENTS

Your final option for starting a new document is to begin from scratch with a blank document. You can do this by selecting <u>Blank Document</u> from the opening <u>PowerPoint</u> dialog, clicking on the <u>New Document</u> icon at the left-hand edge of the main toolbar or selecting the <u>Blank Presentation</u> from the <u>General</u> tab of the <u>New Presentation</u> dialog box. Blank documents, unsurprisingly, come without any pre-set design styles, graphics or textual contents.

A blank title slide, with placeholders.

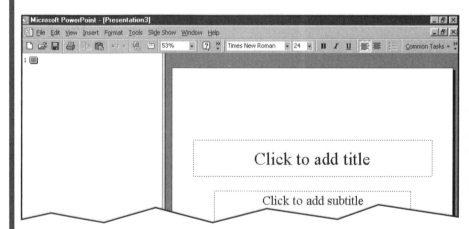

SLIDE AUTOLAYOUTS

Whether you are working with design templates or a blank document, you will need to select a Slide AutoLayout. As mentioned briefly earlier, there are 24 different slide AutoLayout templates that PowerPoint knows. These are absolutely non-negotiable; you cannot modify them or add to them, and every slide has to begin as one of them. This is not particularly restrictive, although it may sound like it at first. Once the slide has been created, all the items on it can be modified, deleted or added to with absolute flexibility, and with a little work you can use any of the different slide types as any of the others. Note that if you delete the slide's title – or start with the blank slide – and later want to add a title, you will need to click next to that slide's image in the Outline box and type a new title manually. You can also re-apply any slide AutoLayout to a slide at any time, as we'll discuss later.

WHAT SLIDE AUTOLAYOUTS ARE AVAILABLE?

There are 24 different slide AutoLayouts, shown below. Tables, charts, org charts, clip art, objects and media clips all need to be created, which we'll look at in detail later on. They are all easy to master, however. Titles, subtitles and text are all just click-and-type, although all the text boxes are formatted as bullet lists by default. You can alter this easily, of course, and we'll look at text formatting in the next chapter. The slides you're likely to use most often are the ones called **Title Slide, Bulleted List, Title Only** and **Blank**. Note that in the image below, a grey bar at the top of the AutoLayout picture represents a title. Only the **Blank** and **Large Object** slides do not have titles.

The full selection of Slide Autolayouts that are available in PowerPoint.

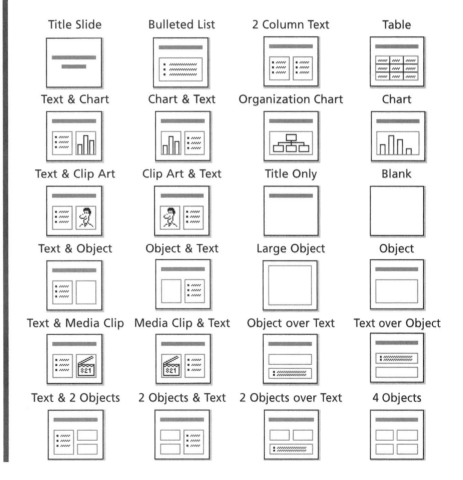

DIFFERENT VIEWS

There are several different ways of examining your presentation in PowerPoint, corresponding to the different ways that the program has of dealing with your slides. Over the next few pages, we'll take a look at the main options you have for changing the way your presentation is displayed while you work.

The Normal View (top). Its icon is on the left-hand side of the View Icons (above).

NORMAL VIEW

The default option for looking at your slides is Normal View. In this view style, your slide takes up about two-thirds of the available screen area. The left-hand side of the screen is reserved for the Outline, which tracks your slides title by title, also displaying subtitles where available, and text boxes created with the AutoLayout. The section at the bottom of the screen shows you any speaker's notes associated with that slide.

SWITCHING VIEWS

The most effective way of switching between different view styles is with the View icons, found towards the bottom left corner of your screen, at the bottom of the Slide Outline area. These five icons, shown below, let you swap between, respectively, Normal View, Outline View, Slide View, Slide Sorter View and the Slide Show. You can also select from Normal View, Slide Sorter View or the Slide Show, and the additional Notes Page view, from the VIEW menu.

Different views: The Slide Outline view with slide details collapsed (above left) and expanded (above right) and the Slide Sorter view (below).

SLIDE VIEW & OUTLINE VIEW

In PowerPoint 2000, the old Slide View – which shows just the slides – and Outline View – which shows only a thumbnail of each slide – are combined into the new Normal View. You can no longer access either of them from the VIEW menu without customization, only from the View icons. If you do need greater detail on your slides or your outline, you can use these icons to select the view you need just by clicking on them.

SLIDE SORTER VIEW

The Slide Sorter lets you get an extended overview of your presentation and manipulate the order in which the slides appear quickly and easily. In addition to being able to drag-and-drop, insert and delete slides, the Slide Sorter view also provides you with a handy toolbar that lets you set transitions, animations, narration, notes and other advanced slide-show functions easily. Slideshow timings, transitions and animations are indicated in the slideshow view beneath the appropriate slides, along with slide numbers. These more advanced topics will be fully explained later in the book.

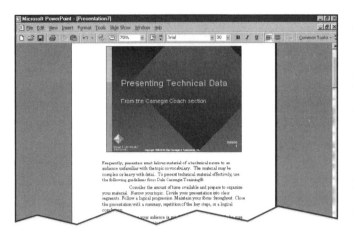

NOTES PAGE VIEW

The Notes Page layout shows each slide compressed into the top half of a sheet of vertically-aligned paper, with the bottom half of the sheet containing the speaker's notes associated with each slide. It is designed to provide easy access to presentation notes that can be referred to in an effective way during a speech itself, but it can also be used equally successfully to create a set of hand-outs to accompany a presentation, (although obviously in this instance the notes you write to accompany each slide will have to be more carefully checked for clarity and spelling than if they were just for personal reference). You can type and edit notes in the Notes Page View too, by clicking on the area underneath the slide and using the text box there as normal. You cannot edit the slide, however.

The Notes Page view (above) and using View Miniature (below).

OTHER VIEWING OPTIONS

If you want to concentrate on the contents of each slide once you have set your design up, you can select Black & White from the VIEW menu. In this mode, slide backgrounds and most Master Slide image objects are omitted from the view, and remaining items are shown in greyscale. This can make it easier to work with slide elements. You can also open a popup image of the slide as it normally appears by selecting View Miniature from the VIEW menu. You may need to click on the down-arrows at the bottom of the menu to display the View Miniature option.

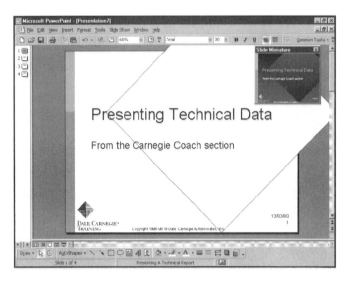

SLIDE DATA

3

While PowerPoint is geared towards the visual presentation of information, the most fundamental component of any slide is generally still the text that it contains. Using the program, you can make your text truly eye-catching, producing a stunning impact with a bare minimum of effort. In this chapter we'll look at the different components that go into making a slide, from titles to tables.

SLIDE ELEMENTS

From PowerPoint's internal viewpoint, a slide is basically a collection of similar objects, each with their own specific sizes, characteristics and positions. Some of these have no borders or internal fills, and contain text; others are graphical; still more are linked externally to other sub-components of the Microsoft Office, or to entirely separate programs. Over the next few pages, we'll have a look at the different elements that slides can contain.

This is a title

☀ This is the first item in a bullet list.
☀ This is the second.
☀ The template for this slide is Cactus, by the way.

WHAT MAKES UP A SLIDE?

A slide consists of several different classes of object. First of all, it takes its initial appearance from a Master slide; any object on the Master will appear as the backdrop for the slide by default. It then has a background area that can contain a solid-colour fill, a pattern, a texture or an image. If a background is set on a slide, it will take priority over the Master slide. After the background come the user objects, the various graphs, charts, drawing objects and text boxes that you create on the slide. Finally, the slide has an Outline area, which holds the text areas provided by the Slide AutoLayout – the title of the slide, for example. In addition, outside of this chain of layers, the slide is also associated with a text box for Speaker's Notes that is not found on the slide itself, and with slideshow details of timing, transitions and animations, which we'll discuss later.

PLACEHOLDERS

When you choose a slide from the AutoLayout, you will see a selection of dotted outline boxes saying things like "Click to add title" or "Double-click to add chart". These are known as placeholders, because they show you the position that the elements they are naming – a title, some text, and so on – will take up on the slide. Placeholders are neither printed on hard copies of slides nor shown during on-screen slide shows, so if you want to leave one blank, you can.

The placeholder ("Click to add title") in the picture on the right does not display in the slideshow shown below.

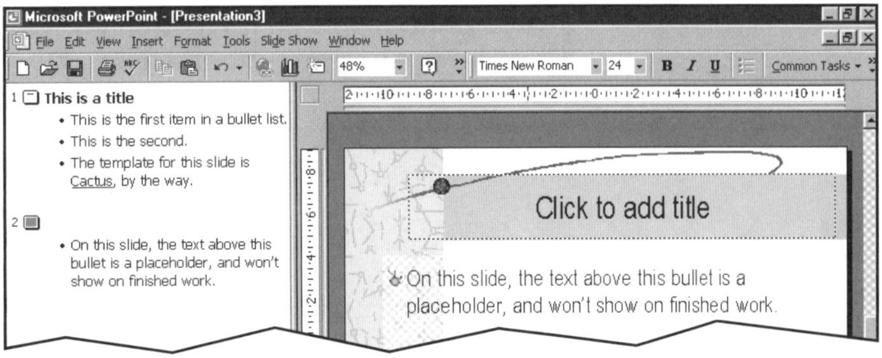

You don't have to use the placeholder elements if you do not want to. They can be moved, resized and deleted in exactly the same way that an object you had personally created can be, and in fact, if you so wish, you can delete all the placeholders on a slide and replace them with identical items from the INSERT menu. Their main purpose is to provide you with guidelines for creating balanced, visually appealing slides. In addition, as discussed earlier, only text entered into a placeholder box is recognised by the Outline, so if you want to keep an accurate record of your slide contents you will have to work with placeholder text boxes. Over the next few pages, we'll look at the different placeholder elements.

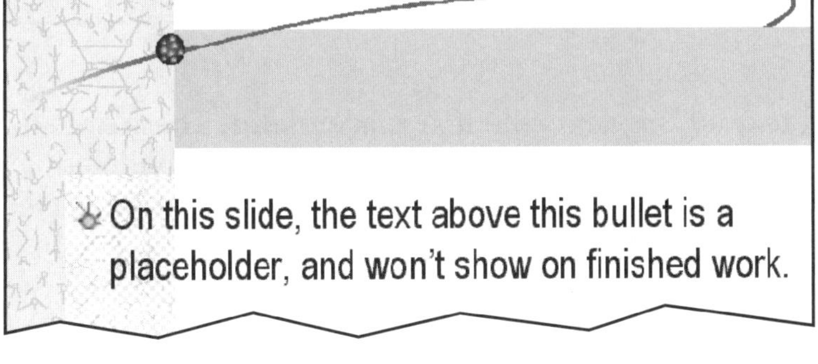

TEXTUAL PLACEHOLDERS

There are three different text-based placeholders available to you. The absolute standard is the slide's title. This is the name which the Outline stores for the slide, and each of them has one. Even the slide types with no title placeholder, the Blank and Large Object slides, still have a title field in the Outline; it's just empty. Confusingly, the Title slide is something different – an introductory slide for your presentation. The Title slide does have a title; it also has a subtitle (the second text-based placeholder), and, with some prepared presentations, its own separate master style. The Title slide is the only one with a subtitle field.

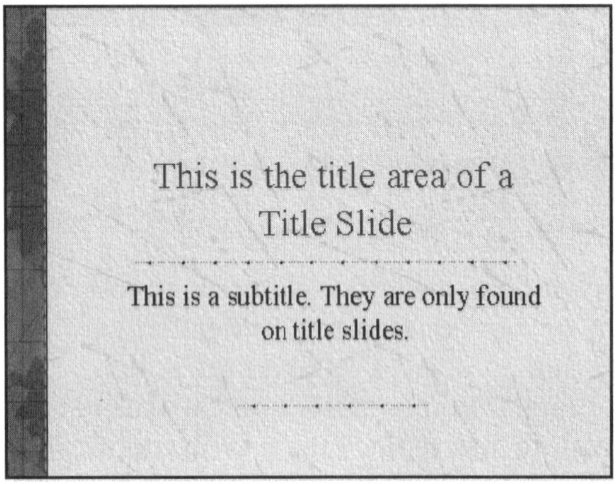

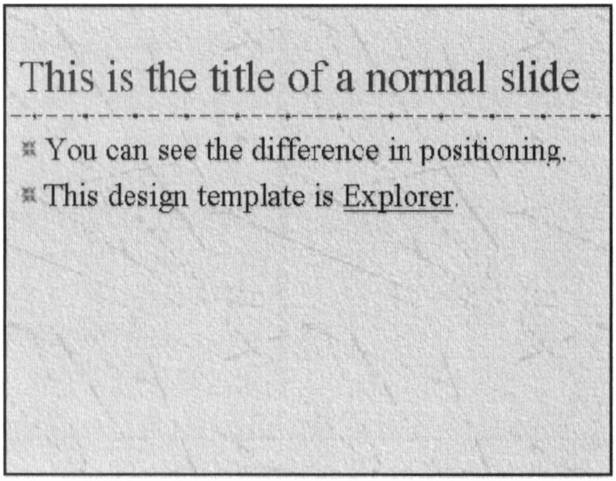

Different design templates have different preset positions for placeholders, carefully balanced to fit in with their designs.

The third textual pre-set is the text placeholder. These are all bullet lists by default; there is no option for a non-bulleted placeholder text field. This doesn't mean that you're restricted to just lists in the Outline, though. Like everything else, you can change the formatting of the text once you've selected the item or started typing in it.

CHART PLACEHOLDERS

Microsoft Graph is an optional Office 2000 component that is designed to make a quick and easy job of preparing all sorts of charts for you. It is based around the charting functions in Excel, and so will be very familiar to you if you know that product. Although it will be present in almost all installations of Microsoft Office, if it is absent you might need to insert your Office 2000 disk to use it, or even run the Office 2000 setup program to install it manually. When you double-click a chart placeholder, PowerPoint will switch to the Microsoft Graph icons and menus, and present you with a datasheet for formatting your chart. Dummy data for a sample bar chart is entered by default, but all the details are, of course, easy to change. We'll look at the details of preparing charts in the next chapter.

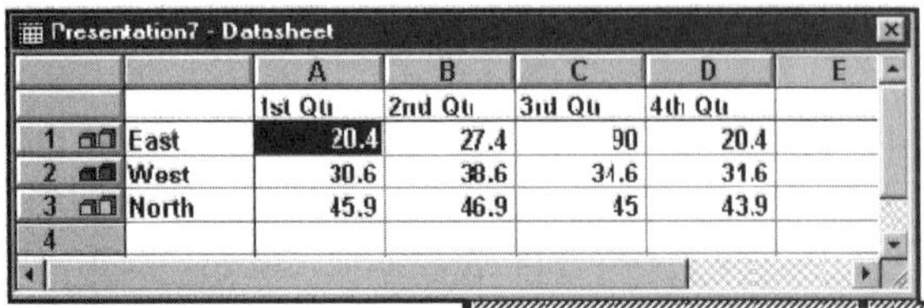

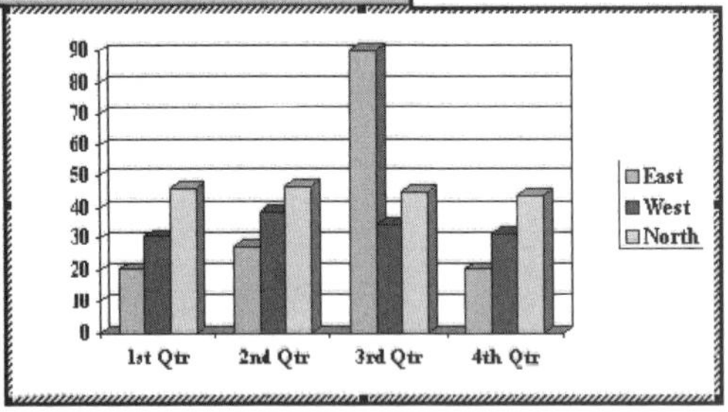

Default Microsoft Graph datasheet (above) and output (right) give you something to work with when designing a chart.

ORGANIZATION CHART PLACEHOLDERS

Org charts are a way of tracking the management structure of a company or other structured group. Lines of responsibility and seniority run from the head of the company down through their chains of command to front-line staff. Double-clicking the org chart placeholder opens the Microsoft Organization Chart program, and provides you with a window holding a dummy organizational structure for you to modify. The details of how to prepare an org chart are covered in the next chapter.

Microsoft Organization Chart's initial defaults.

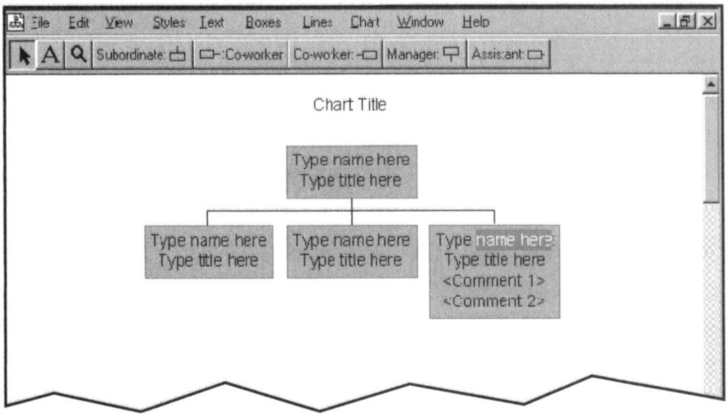

CLIP ART AND MEDIA CLIP PLACEHOLDERS

Double-clicking the Clip Art or Media Clip placeholder opens the Microsoft Clip Gallery, from which you can choose a piece of Clip Art (or a movie file for Media Clips) to insert into your presentation. Simple, colourful pictures across a wide range of subject areas, Clip Art images are used to liven up a presentation or illustrate a point. Traditionally, Clip Art images are copyright-free, so you can use them for any purpose, according to your needs. We'll look at the details of working with Clip Art later.

A Clip Art illustration in place.

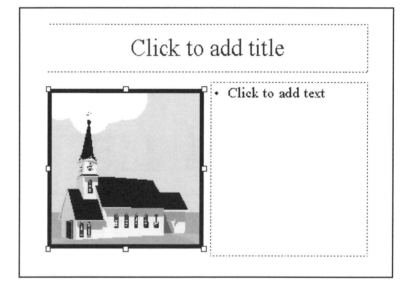

OBJECT PLACEHOLDERS

An Object is, specifically, a document created by one program that is inserted into a document in a different program. Objects commonly found in PowerPoint slides include Microsoft Excel spreadsheets, Microsoft Access databases, Photoshop images and so on. When you edit an Object, the program that created it is opened to let you work on it. Technically speaking, Charts, Org Charts, Clip Art and Media Clips are all Objects, and you can use an Object placeholder to create any of them if you so wish. We'll go into more detail on Objects later.

TABLE PLACEHOLDERS

A table is a rectangular grid of boxes, referred to as cells. Each horizontal line of cells is known as a row, and each vertical line is a column. Tables are used to present categorised data in a structured manner, particularly numerical information, so that it can be cross-referenced. In other words, each row generally represents one individual item in a list, and each column represents a category that the individual has relevant information for. If you were arranging sales figures, for example, you might list one salesperson on each row, and have the columns representing their performances on each month of the year. To help make things clear, it is usual to use the first row and the first column for titles, as below:

The first row and the first column of the table hold titles.

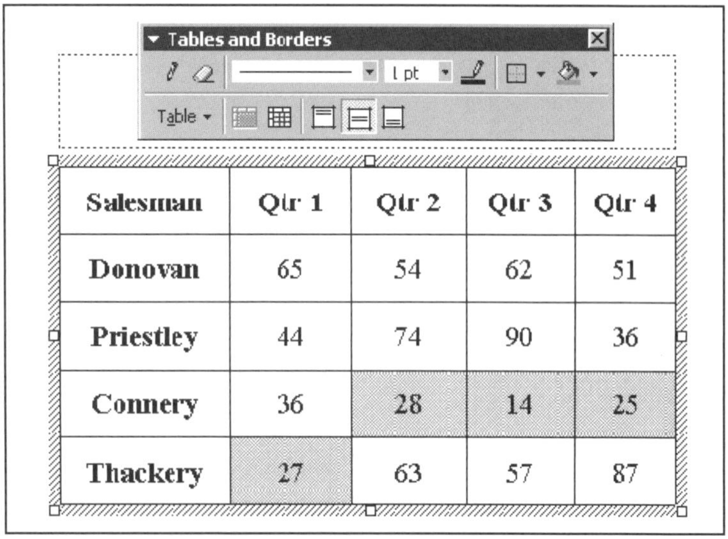

Salesman	Qtr 1	Qtr 2	Qtr 3	Qtr 4
Donovan	65	54	62	51
Priestley	44	74	90	36
Connery	36	28	14	25
Thackery	27	63	57	87

The tables you can draw in PowerPoint are simple grids of lines with text boxes inside them. While they are extremely flexible, other programs in Microsoft Office – notably Excel – provide considerably more sophisticated ways of working with tables, allowing you to perform calculations with different cells, cross-reference information and program all sorts of complex functions. If you need to use a sophisticated table like this in your presentation, you should create an Object based on a Microsoft Excel spreadsheet.

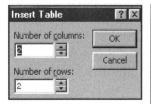

DRAWING A TABLE
Drawing a table in PowerPoint is easy, whether you use a placeholder or not.

1 To start a table, double-click on a table placeholder or select Table from the INSERT menu. The Insert Table dialog box will appear, asking you to enter the number of rows and columns in the table. Type in the values you want and click OK...

2 ...OR you can click on the Table icon on the main toolbar to bring up a grid of cells. Dragging within that grid will let you choose the number of rows and columns for your table – the dark area on the grid – and they are also shown at the bottom of the grid. Click the mouse (or, if you are click-dragging, release it) to insert the table.

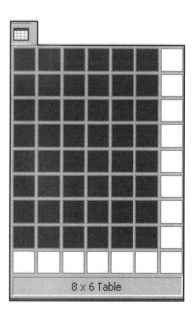

3 Your table will be inserted on the slide – inside the placeholder if that's what you used, or centred on the slide if you did not use a placeholder.

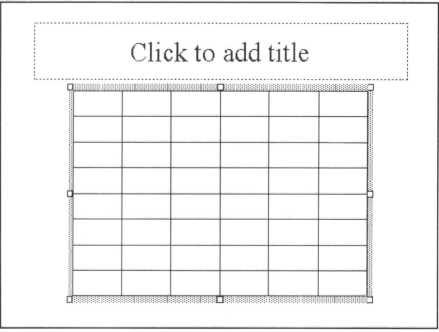

The <u>Tables and Borders</u> toolbar gives you easy access to table formatting.

FORMATTING A TABLE

Tables are formatted using the <u>Tables and Borders</u> toolbar, which should appear whenever you select a table. If it does not, select <u>Tables and Borders</u> from the <u>Toolbars</u> submenu of the <u>VIEW</u> menu.

You can add rows and columns, or even divide selections of cells, with the <u>Draw Table</u> pencil-like icon. When you click on this button, you can click and drag to draw lines that the Table will straighten up for you and turn into cell dividers. The <u>Eraser</u> icon next to it will delete a line you click on, merging the cell with the one next to it. You can merge a whole straight line of cells. If the cells cannot merge – if you try to merge round a corner, for example – only the cell's border line will be removed instead. You can select a new <u>Line Style</u>, <u>Line Weight</u> and <u>Border Colour</u> from the next three icons; these will apply to the next line(s) you draw, or to the next border you apply, which is done from the box-shaped icon next to the line colour tool. Set the styling you want, select a cell and click on the down-arrow next to the border box icon to get a droplist of border lines to apply the style to – from just one side of the cell through to all borders, external and internal. If the border box is already set to the border(s) you want to change, just click on it and the style will be applied to the chosen borders of the selected cells.

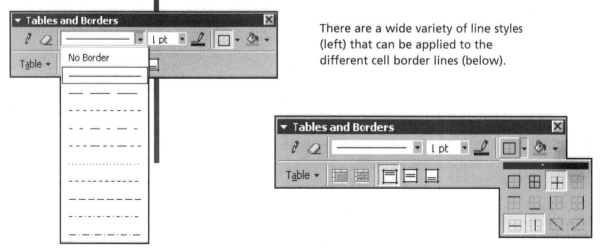

There are a wide variety of line styles (left) that can be applied to the different cell border lines (below).

More advanced options are available to you from the <u>Table</u> menu, obtained by clicking on the <u>Table</u> menu button on the bottom left of the <u>Tables and Borders</u> bar. The two buttons next to it, <u>Merge Cells</u> and <u>Split Cell</u> respectively, allow you to combine two or more cells into one larger one (removing the internal borders), or break a cell into two smaller ones.

From this menu bar, you can insert or delete rows and columns, merge or split cells, select an entire row, column or table, insert a new table or call up a <u>Borders and Fill</u> formatting dialog box, which gives you finer control over the process of formatting the selected cells.

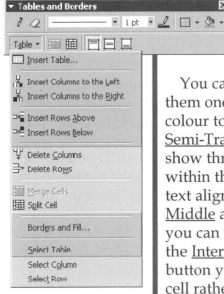

Advanced table manipulation options are available from the <u>Table</u> menu.

You can select line styles, colours and weights and apply them one by one from the <u>Borders</u> tab, select a background colour to fill the cell from on the <u>Fill</u> tab – note that ticking the <u>Semi-Transparent</u> option box allows the slide background to show through the cell fill – or select the positioning of the text within the cell from the <u>Text Box</u> tab. As well as the way the text aligns in the cell, which can also be set from the <u>Top</u>, <u>Middle</u> and <u>Bottom</u> buttons on the <u>Tables and Borders</u> bar, you can also set how close the text comes to the cell walls with the <u>Internal Margin</u> options, and if you tick the <u>Rotate Text...</u> button you can choose to have the cell's text read down the cell rather than across it. When you have set the options you want to use, click <u>Preview</u> to see how they will look on the table itself, or <u>OK</u> to actually apply them.

The <u>Format Table</u> dialog box gives you detailed control.

GETTING A PLACEHOLDER

If you want to add a placeholder to a slide, you need to reapply a slide AutoLayout. When you do this, PowerPoint will attempt to make sense of items you already have on the slide in terms of the layout you are applying. This may result in your text or diagrams shifting position somewhat if the layout you apply is different to the one you applied initially, or if you moved your placeholders. If PowerPoint cannot sensibly reposition an element on your slide in terms of the AutoLayout, it will just leave it where it is. Applying an AutoLayout is easy.

1 From the FORMAT menu, select Slide Layout…, or click on the Common Tasks button on the main toolbar and select Slide Layout from the drop-down pick list.

2 The Slide Layout dialog box will appear, with your slide's current AutoLayout selected. Either click on the Reapply button to re-use the current AutoLayout, or select a different layout and click on the button, which now reads Apply.

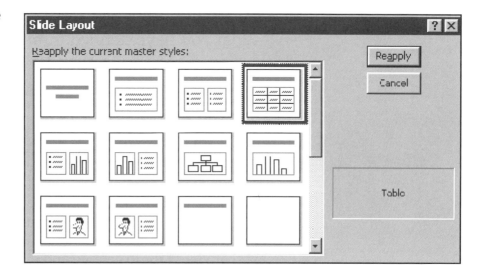

3 Your slide will be formatted to the selected AutoLayout.

FITTING TEXT

If you type more text into a placeholder than there is room for on the screen, PowerPoint will try to make the text fit by changing line spacing or shrinking the text. If you do not want it to do this, you can disable it by selecting Options from the TOOLS menu, clicking the Edit tab and then clearing the Auto-fit text to text placeholder check box.

FORMATTING TEXT

Although PowerPoint goes to great pains to offer you a range of pre-designed styles and templates that have been carefully balanced for maximum impact and readability, sometimes you will want to use text styles that you have defined. It may be that your work needs to match a particular in-house style, or you may want to get a type of effect that PowerPoint does not cater for. In this section, we'll show you how to modify the way your text appears on the screen.

CHANGING FONT

The most basic piece of styling information is the font that your text is displayed in. A font is a set of letters and numbers that are designed in a similar manner. To change font, select the text that you want to change and click on the down arrow at the edge of the <u>Font</u> box, shown below. Scroll through the list of fonts until you find one that you want, and then click on it. It will be selected, and the text will change. The new version of PowerPoint shows you the font names displayed in their own font, so you can see the effect you will achieve.

CHANGING FONT STYLES

The <u>Font Size</u> box and the three icons (<u>Bold</u>, <u>Italic</u> and <u>Underline</u>) immediately to the right of the <u>Font</u> box are used for changing certain aspects of the way that your data is displayed. These are known as different styles of the basic font. Normal text – the way that this sentence is displayed – is referred to as Roman, and it is the conventional way of displaying printed text. The most common alternatives to Roman are to use a **bold piece of text like this**, or to set text *as italics like this*. Both are used to draw attention to information; bold text usually means something is important or particularly significant, while italics usually mean something is explanatory or should be spoken with emphasis. These usages vary, though. A fourth option is to combine both ***as bold italics, like this***. This is less common, and looks vaguely frantic. With the third icon, you can also choose to <u>underline a piece of text like this</u>, including <u>**bold**</u>, <u>*italics*</u> and <u>***bold italics***</u>. Simply select the piece of text that you want to modify and click on one or more of the <u>Bold</u>, <u>Italic</u> or <u>Underline</u> icons shown below.

Font Name, Point Size, Bold, Italic, Underline.

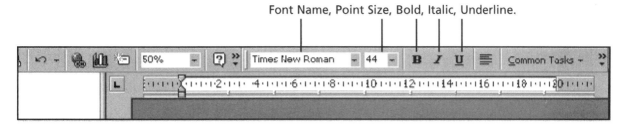

The <u>Formatting</u> toolbar begins with the Font Name dropdown menu.

The other basic change you can make to your normal font style is to alter the size of the letters themselves. This is called the point size, and is abbreviated to pt. The smaller the point size, the smaller the letters are. In books and letters, most normal text is displayed between 8pt – which looks like this – and 14pt – which looks like this. In PowerPoint, titles are generally 44pt, and subtitles and bullet lists are 32pt. Select the text you want to modify, and use the <u>Font Size</u> box shown above – either click on it and type in your new point size between 1pt and 4000pt (although we would recommend not going much higher than 500pt text), or click on the down-arrow and select a new point size from the drop-down list.

FONT EFFECTS

There are a range of other font effects that you can apply to your selected text swiftly and easily.

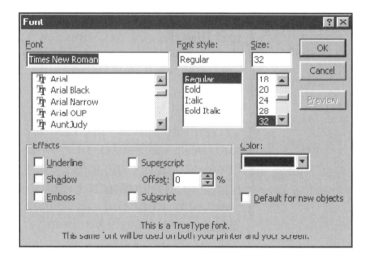

1 From the FORMAT menu, select Font.

2 The Font dialog box will appear. As well as menus to select the various font styling options, you will also see a group of tick boxes for the various font effects, and a drop-down pick list box for font colour.

This is shadowed

This is embossed

The last word is superscript

The last word is subscript

This line is grey

3 Select the effects you wish to apply. You can then click on the Preview button to see how they will look, or OK to apply them. You cannot choose both Embossing and Shadow at the same time, and you cannot choose both Subscript and Superscript at the same time. The Offset box tells PowerPoint by how much to raise or lower the text from the standard base line for custom subscript and superscript. Examples are shown here.

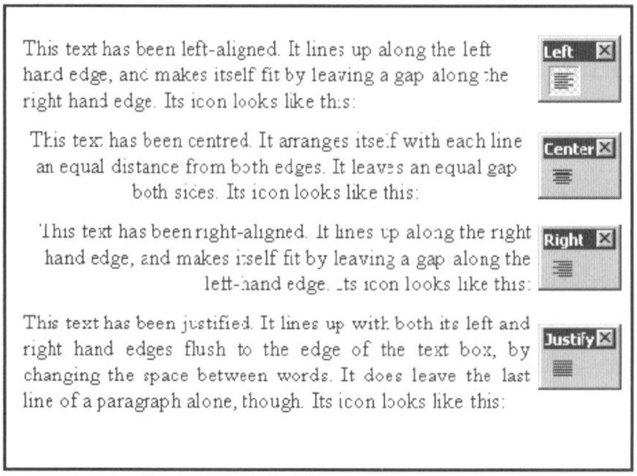

This text has been left-aligned. It lines up along the left hand edge, and makes itself fit by leaving a gap along the right hand edge. Its icon looks like this:

This text has been centred. It arranges itself with each line an equal distance from both edges. It leaves an equal gap both sides. Its icon looks like this:

This text has been right-aligned. It lines up along the right hand edge, and makes itself fit by leaving a gap along the left-hand edge. Its icon looks like this:

This text has been justified. It lines up with both its left and right hand edges flush to the edge of the text box, by changing the space between words. It does leave the last line of a paragraph alone, though. Its icon looks like this:

ALIGNMENT AND OTHER OPTIONS

There are several ways that text can be lined up on the page. This is referred to as alignment. PowerPoint prefers to handle text alignment for you by default, so the icons are hidden in the More Buttons box, and the Alignment submenu from the FORMAT menu will at first not be visible until you click on the down-arrows at the bottom of the menu, expanding it, and select Alignment. There are four alignments to choose from. Click in the text you want to align, or select it, and pick an alignment as described above.

Other options you have for changing the way text is displayed include an automatic function to reapply a case to the text you have selected, by choosing Change Case… from the FORMAT menu (like Alignment, not visible until you click on the down-arrows at the bottom of the menu), and a dialog box to let you modify the space between the lines of your text from the also-hidden Line Spacing… option on the FORMAT menu. As well as changing the gap between each line, you can add a line gap to the start and/or end of a paragraph of text.

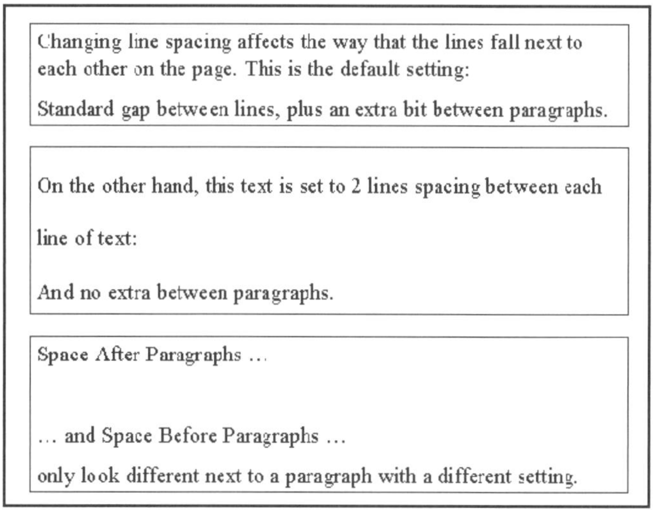

Changing line spacing affects the way that the lines fall next to each other on the page. This is the default setting:

Standard gap between lines, plus an extra bit between paragraphs.

On the other hand, this text is set to 2 lines spacing between each

line of text:

And no extra between paragraphs.

Space After Paragraphs …

… and Space Before Paragraphs …

only look different next to a paragraph with a different setting.

Examples of different types of line spacing.

1 To alter tabs or indents, you need to have the horizontal ruler visible. Select <u>Ruler</u> from the <u>VIEW</u> menu. You'll have to click on the down-arrows at the bottom of the menu to reveal it as an option the first time.

TABS, INDENTS AND LISTS

Tab stops are a way of lining text up in an orderly fashion on the page. When you press the tab key (called *inserting a tab*), the cursor immediately jumps to the next tab stop. The default style for text boxes and titles is for tab stops to be positioned an inch apart, although you can add tabs manually. Indents are like tab stops, but they apply to all text, and specify how close to the left-hand edge the text is. A full indent affects all text, but it is easier to move the left side of the text box. First-line indents and hanging indents are more useful, though. A first line indent, as it suggests, indents just the first line of a paragraph. A hanging indent indents every line except the first.

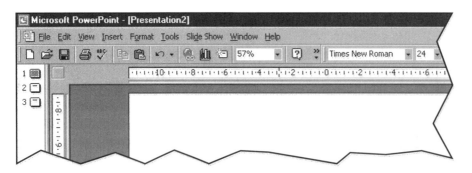

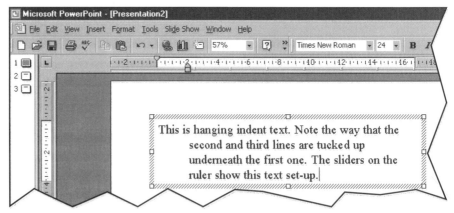

2 Indents are controlled with the little slider at the left of the white part of the ruler. Look at it closely. The rectangular pad at the bottom sets the overall indent. The lower triangular pad sets the hanging indent, and the upper triangular pad sets the first-line indent. It will always indicate (and modify) the settings for the currently-selected text.

3 Default tab stops are controlled from the tiny notches along the bottom of the ruler. Click and slide one to set the space between each default tab stop. You can also add one or more manual tab stops. A manual tab stop will replace all the default tabs between itself and the left-hand edge. Click on the ruler to add a manual tab stop at that position.

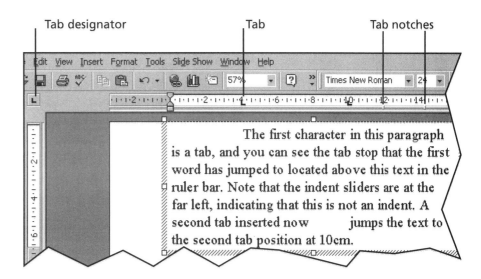

Tab designator   Tab   Tab notches

The first character in this paragraph is a tab, and you can see the tab stop that the first word has jumped to located above this text in the ruler bar. Note that the indent sliders are at the far left, indicating that this is not an indent. A second tab inserted now   jumps the text to the second tab position at 10cm.

You can move a manual tab stop by clicking and dragging it to a new position, or remove it by dragging it off the ruler altogether. The standard setting for a tab stop is left-align; that is, the text after the inserted tab starts to the left of the tab stop. You can also have centred tab stops, where the text is centred on the tab stop, right-align tab stops, where the right-hand edge of the text ends on the tab stop, and decimal stops (used for a column of figures) where the text is centred on the first period character (a '.') in the text. Clicking on the Tab Stop Type box to the left of the ruler will cycle through the four different types in the order given above. When it shows the type of tab stop you want, clicking on the ruler will apply that type of manual tab stop at that position.

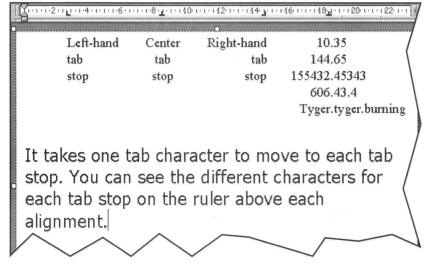

Left-hand	Center	Right-hand	10.35
tab	tab	tab	144.65
stop	stop	stop	155432.45343
			606.43.4
			Tyger.tyger.burning

It takes one tab character to move to each tab stop. You can see the different characters for each tab stop on the ruler above each alignment.

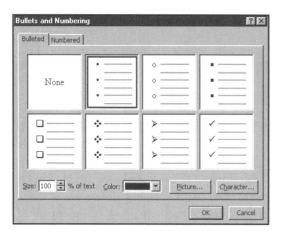

BULLET LISTS AND NUMBER LISTS

As we discussed earlier, PowerPoint by default sets all text as a bullet list, with a half-line space after each paragraph. It also calculates a hanging indent for your text that is large enough to provide space for a standard bullet character. When a bullet list is applied, PowerPoint considers the bullet character to be the first line, so the next character – the start of your text – is indented to the hanging indent position. You can change your bullet character (or switch to a numbered list) by selecting <u>Bullets and Numbering…</u> from the <u>FORMAT</u> menu.

You can select one of the default bullet shapes from the <u>Bullets</u> tab, or click on the <u>Numbers</u> tab to get a list of different numbered list styles you can select from. You can also pick any character from any font as a bullet from the <u>Character…</u> button, or a clip-art image from the <u>Picture…</u> button. You can also set the colour of the bullet and its size relative to the text from both tabs, and on the <u>Numbers</u> tab you have the option of starting (or restarting if you select a line part-way down a list) from a number other than 1.

Different Bullet Options Include:

- A standard bullet…
- …that should look pretty familiar.
- ❖ A different standard option, coloured red.

ii. One of the numbered…
iii. …bullet selections…
iv. …starting from 2.

- ▣ Finally, a picture bullet from clip art…
- © …and a character bullet.

SWITCHING BULLETS ON AND OFF

If you want, you can remove or add text bulleting. To remove bullets that are active, or to insert bullets to normal text, click on the <u>Bullets</u> icon on the <u>Formatting</u> tool bar – hidden in the <u>More Buttons</u> box before its first use, so you'll have to click on the right-arrows at the end of the tool bar. You will need to modify the hanging indent in either instance, though, so it's easier to use placeholders for bullet text and text boxes for non-bullet text. The icon looks like this:

SLIDE GRAPHICS

4

Although it has excellent text-handling functions, PowerPoint really comes alive with its simple, convenient graphical manipulation abilities. It is extremely easy to add effective images to a PowerPoint document. In this chapter we'll look at creating and modifying the visual components that go into a presentation, including charts, clip art, pictures, org charts, AutoShapes and WordArt. We'll also discuss how to format objects, from border lines to textures, and consider the use of Master slides to apply a consistent look and feel to your presentation.

VISUAL OBJECTS

Referring to 'visual' objects is something of a false distinction in PowerPoint. In many senses, everything on a PowerPoint slide is treated in the same way. However, it is useful to contrast different groups of item that behave in a similar way. In this section, we'll look at the group made up of graphs, organization charts and Clip Art – all three are external to the true PowerPoint program, but are key parts of most presentations and have their own specific short-cuts on the Slide AutoLayouts. We'll also check out WordArt – although it doesn't have its own special placeholder on the AutoLayouts, it too is an Office-standard external program.

A Microsoft
Graph object.

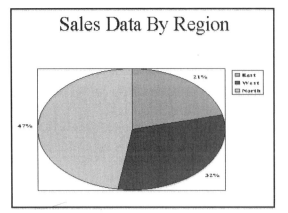

DIFFERENT TYPES OF OBJECT

The word 'Object' seems obvious enough, but has several different meanings. To programmers, an object is a document from one program that is linked – *embedded* – into another program. This is achieved by a piece of Windows' internal software called OLE, Object Linking and Embedding. What it means in practice is that you can use one program to produce some output – a graph, an equation, whatever – then show it inside

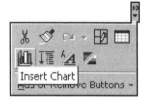

a different program, such as on a PowerPoint Slideshow, yet still be able to edit it from its original program. Charts, org charts, WordArt and Clip Art are all Objects in this sense – they are created outside PowerPoint, and linked into your slide. All sorts of other programs can be linked in too, but we'll look at them later on in the book.

1 You can click on the Insert Chart icon on the main tool bar...

CREATING A CHART

The easy way of inserting a chart, of course, is to double-click on a chart placeholder. We've already covered placeholders in quite a lot of depth, though, so for the rest of this chapter we're going to assume that you know all about getting the placeholders you need, and not worry further about them. Instead, we'll look at the alternative, manual methods of doing things, because although they're slightly less convenient, they are a lot more flexible.

To go about getting the chart you want, enter your data over the top of the datasheet box. You can see from the default that each column of the datasheet corresponds to an item on the X-axis of the chart, and that each row represents the Y-axis values. The first row and column respectively provide titles. There are many different charts styles available, so don't fear that you're stuck with the basic one.

2 ... or you can select Chart... from the INSERT menu.

3 In either case, a chart box is created in the area which the Master slide defines as being for AutoLayouts. The Microsoft Graph program, which handles the chart creation, inserts a default chart into the space to help guide you.

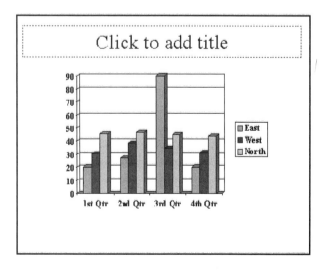

PREPARING A CHART

Once you've entered the correct data into the datasheet – the data should start in the cell in Column A and Row 1, or A1, with text headings in the unlabeled row and column – you can set about preparing the type of chart you actually want. It is considered standard to have a series of data in one row, with the different columns representing the category values. In other words, if you have just one set of data – percentage responses to a question in a survey, for example – it should all be in one row. While the chart is being edited, the usual PowerPoint menus and toolbars are replaced with those of Microsoft Graph, which is in the driving seat. To actually choose the type of chart you wish to display your data in, select Chart Type... from the CHART menu.

You can select from a wide range of different chart styles using the Chart Type dialog box. Click on the general type you want, and then on one of the sub-types that appears in the right-hand area of the screen. To see how your current set of data would look using that type of chart, click on the Press and Hold to View Sample button. There are a number of specialized charts also available on the Custom Types tab. A description of the chart's use and other notes appears below the sub-types menu.

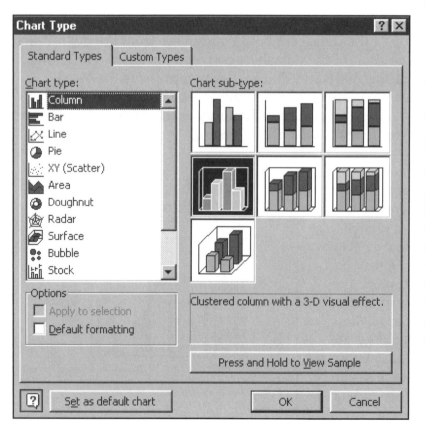

A wide range of different chart types are available.

FORMATTING A CHART

Once the basic layout has been chosen, there are a number of options that you can set for the chart. Selecting Chart Options… from the CHART menu opens the Chart Options dialog box. From this, you can set all sorts of options, depending on the chart type. Assuming the chart supports all the various options, you can title it – and its various axes – via the Titles tab, turn the axes themselves on and off from the Axes tab, turn chart grid lines on and off from the Gridlines tab, activate and/or position the explanatory legend box from the Legend tab, display exact figures on the chart with the Data Labels tabs, and show a copy of the data itself below the chart with the Data Table tab. The more options you set, however, the smaller your actual chart area will be.

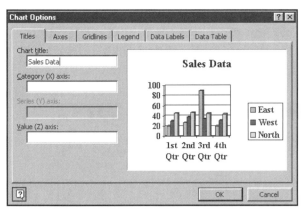

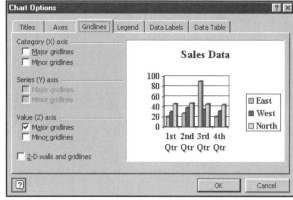

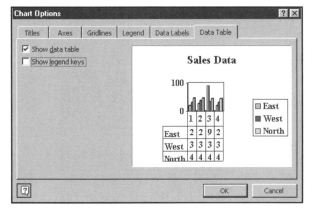

The different tabs of the Chart Options dialog box give you access to a great variety of informational tools for labelling your chart.

CHART ELEMENTS

In addition to the chart options, each element of the chart can be individually formatted, from the background of the chart area to the axis bars. Holding the mouse pointer still over a spot will show you a <u>Tool Tip</u> naming the item you would select by clicking in that position.

When you have the correct point, right-click and select the Format <TYPE>… option from the pick-list. The format boxes are all broadly standard, and different tabs will provide access to all relevant formatting choices, such as font style, colours and fills, labels and so on. There is no room to go into detail here, but they are all fairly self-explanatory. They are based on the Chart routines of Microsoft Excel, so if you have used that program you will find no surprises here. When your chart is ready, click outside the chart box, on the slide background, to return to PowerPoint.

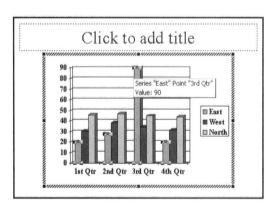

Once your chart is in place you can modify its appearance. The <u>Format</u> dialog box that you receive depends upon which part of the chart is selected.

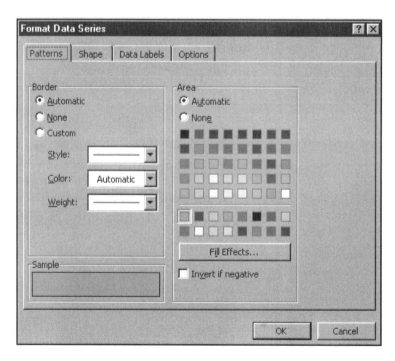

CREATING AN ORGANIZATION CHART

Organization charts, or org charts for short, are used to display the management structure of a company or organisation by illustrating the chain of command.

1 Adding an org chart to your presentation is easy. Highlight Picture on the INSERT menu, and select Organization Chart from the sub-menu that appears.

2 PowerPoint will assign a space for the chart, centred on the middle of the slide, that roughly coincides with the default area for AutoLayout formats. This space is left blank temporarily while you build your chart.

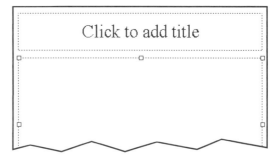

3 At the same time, the Microsoft Organization Chart program is opened in a new floating window. Unlike Microsoft Graph, this program does not take over your PowerPoint menus; it remains entirely

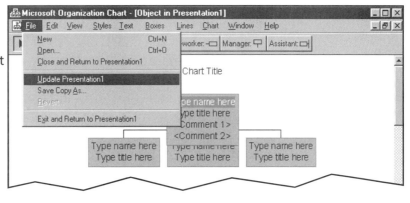

separate. Once you've finished, you should update the org chart in your presentation by clicking Update from the org chart FILE menu before closing Microsoft Graph.

PREPARING AN ORG CHART

Each box in an org chart represents one person, with the top of the chart being the head of the company, organisation or department as appropriate. MS Org Chart starts you off with a simple structure of one manager with three subordinates. If you don't want to work with that structure, you can select a box by clicking on it and then delete it by pressing the <u>Delete</u> key or selecting <u>Clear</u> from the <u>EDIT</u> menu. You cannot easily alter a box's type once it is set, so you may need to delete some of the preset boxes.

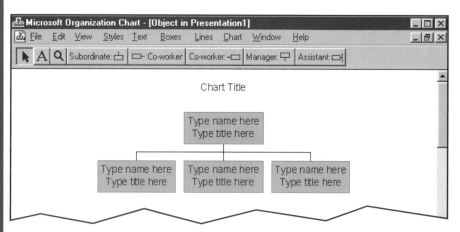

As you'll see in the diagram above, there are five different styles of business relationship represented on the tool bar next to the <u>Select</u> tool, <u>Enter Text</u> tool and <u>Zoom</u> tool icons. To add a new person into the chart, click on a box style and then on a box. A Subordinate will be added below the box, a <u>Manager</u> will be added in the box's current position, moving the box down one row, an <u>Assistant</u> will be added below the box but off to one side and a <u>Co-Worker</u> will be added with the box, jointly subordinate to the box's manager – to the left or the right of the box depending on the icon chosen. Some more complicated business relationships are shown from the <u>STYLES</u> menu; select one or more boxes and click on one of the Styles to apply that particular visual style to the boxes selected. There is no room to go into specific details here, but the program comes with extensive help files if you run into problems.

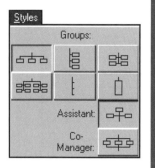

Advanced business relationships are shown in the <u>Styles</u> menu.

FORMATTING AN ORG CHART

The default style for a new org chart created from PowerPoint has green boxes with black text and lines on a white background. This is a slight departure from the program's standard style, which is black and white, with no box fills – as you'll see if you start a <u>New</u> chart from the <u>FILE</u> menu. The formatting options available to you are accessed via the <u>TEXT</u>, <u>BOXES</u>, <u>LINES</u> and <u>CHART</u> menus. The various options apply to the current selection – you can hold <u>Shift</u> down to click multiple selections, or choose a selection option from the <u>Select</u> submenu of the <u>EDIT</u> menu. The <u>TEXT</u> menu offers you dialogs for <u>Font</u>, <u>Color</u> and text alignment within the box. The <u>BOXES</u> menu allows you to set the background and borders of the box. The <u>LINES</u> menu lets you choose line <u>Style</u>, <u>Thickness</u> and <u>Color</u> for the lines connecting boxes. Finally, the <u>CHART</u> menu lets you set a <u>Background Color</u> for the chart. You should note that these options are considerably less sophisticated than PowerPoint's own colour, fill, border and line options.

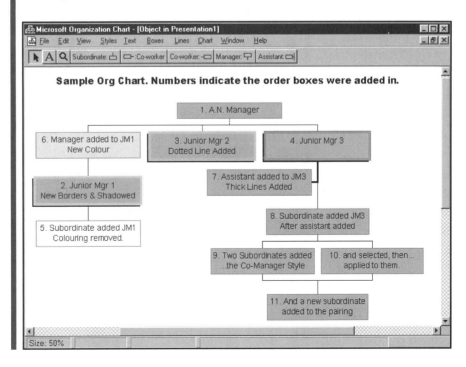

In this sample chart a wide range of formatting options are demonstrated.

THE CLIP ART GALLERY

Clip Art is a generic term for small, illustrative, cartoon-like images provided on an open-copyright basis that can be used to liven up a presentation or other document. Specifically, in Microsoft Office, it means pictures files of this nature inserted from the Clip Art gallery. Microsoft Office Clip Art images are actually made up of a collection of Drawing Objects, so they can be ungrouped and re-coloured, textured, have their shape modified and so on, if needs be – we'll look at working with Drawing Objects later. This differentiates them from standard picture files, which are always treated as one solid, indivisible unit.

1 You can click on the Insert Clip Art icon on the Drawing tool bar at the bottom of the screen to insert a piece of Clip Art...

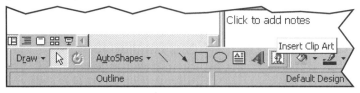

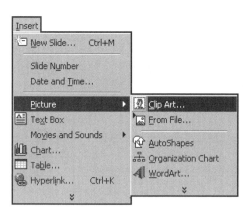

2 ... or you can select Clip Art... from the Picture submenu of the INSERT menu.

3 The Insert Clip Art dialog box, known as the Clip Art Gallery, will appear, giving you a list of Clip Art categories to choose from.

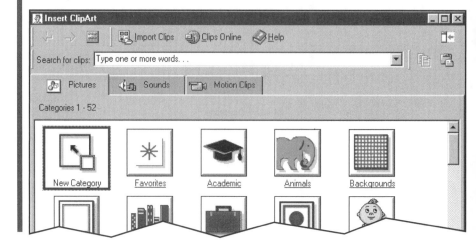

1 When you've found a piece of Clip Art that you like, click on it. A small, speech-bubble shaped dialog box will appear.

SELECTING CLIP ART

The Clip Art Gallery operates rather like a web browser. You select a category of Clip Art by clicking on the image (or name) of the category you want to browse. There are wide range of different categories for you to choose from, and any given piece of Clip Art will be found in all relevant categories – so Recycling is found in Nature as well as in Symbols, for example. You can also use the Back and Forward icons on the Clip Art Gallery main toolbar – they work like a web browser – and you can type a keyword into the Search for Clips box to match all pieces of Clip Art that have that keyword in their definitions.

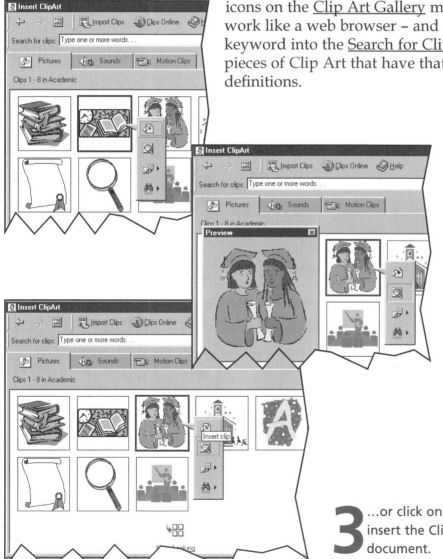

2 You can click on the Preview Clip button to open a larger preview of the clip image...

3 ...or click on the Insert Clip button to insert the Clip Art into your document.

CREATING WORDART

WordArt is an impressive Microsoft Office add-on that lets you turn simple text into one of a range of impressive illustrated styles using a set of templates. It is perfect for informal, high-impact solutions such as posters and banners, or for a slideshow that will be shown to the general public.

1 To create a piece of WordArt, click on the <u>WordArt</u> icon on the <u>Drawing</u> toolbar at the bottom of the screen, or select <u>WordArt...</u> from the <u>Picture</u> submenu of the <u>INSERT</u> menu.

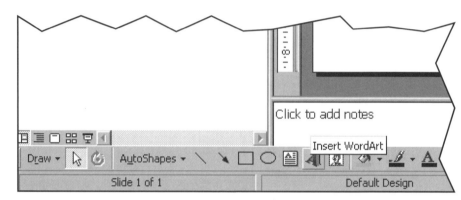

2 The <u>WordArt</u> <u>Gallery</u> dialog box will appear, showing all the different styles of WordArt image available to you. Click on one and press <u>OK</u> to select it. You can change it later if you want to, so you don't need to worry too much about getting it right first time.

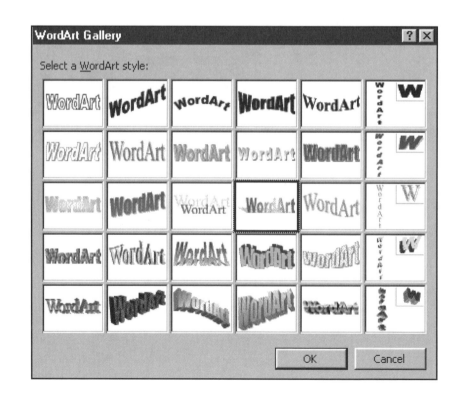

3 In the Edit WordArt Text dialog box, enter the text that you want displayed in WordArt. You can also change the font, the point size and the type style with standard text formatting icons.

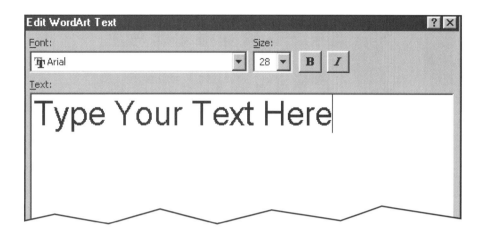

4 Click OK, and your piece of WordArt will be placed on your slide.

5 Whenever the WordArt is selected, the WordArt Floating Toolbar will appear. From this bar, you can format every aspect of the WordArt.

Pay attention to the second button on it, Edit Text, which lets you revise the text of your WordArt, the third button, WordArt Gallery, which lets you choose a different basic style, the fourth button, Format WordArt, which provides access to the Object Formatting options, and the fifth button, WordArt Shape, which lets you change the shape of the text within the context of the gallery style you have chosen.

DRAWING OBJECTS

There is a class of image types known as Drawing Objects. These are, literally, objects that are drawings. Unlike the Visual Objects, though, they do not require the use of an external program to create them. They range from the very simplest lines up to complicated shapes, and provide a powerful way of adding colourful, custom-made illustrations to a slide. In this section, we'll look at the different types of Drawing Objects and getting the most from them.

THE DRAWING TOOLBAR

The most effective way to get access to the various drawing objects and their related functions is through the <u>Drawing Toolbar</u>, which is at the bottom of the screen. The <u>Drawing Toolbar</u> looks like this:

The different Drawing Object types are best accessed from the icons on the toolbar. The first group of buttons on the bar – the <u>DRAW</u> menu, <u>Select Objects</u> icon and <u>Free Rotate</u> tool – provides various object manipulation options. The second group consists of the icons that you use to insert Drawing Objects (<u>AutoShape</u>, line art tools and <u>Text Box</u>), along with <u>WordArt</u> and <u>Clip Art.</u> The third group of icons are all formatting shortcuts.

LINE ART

The most basic method of drawing using PowerPoint is to join several pieces of Line Art. That is, to use the most basic of all possible drawing tools – a rectangle, an oval, a straight line, and an arrow. You can do quite a lot more with these basic items than you may think, including constructing manual charts, frames, simple geometric constructs and more. Pieces of line art, like all Drawing Objects, can be positioned anywhere in your slide, including over other items already in place.

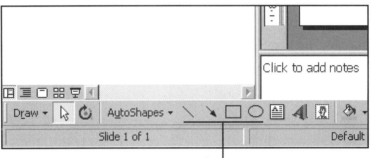

The line art tools.

To use a line art tool, click on it to select it, then click at the start point on your slide and drag until your line art is the right size. Sometimes, you will want to *constrain* the item. Constraining makes Lines and Arrows run parallel to the grid (or at 15 degree intervals to it) or makes the Rectangle and Oval into geometrically 'perfect' shapes – squares and circles respectively. To constrain line art – and AutoShapes – hold down the Shift key before you start drawing and do not release it until after you finish. Similarly, you can make PowerPoint use the point you first clicked on as the center of your line art or AutoShape by pressing Ctrl; otherwise, it will use the point you first clicked on as a corner.

AUTOSHAPES

In addition to the simple design and drawing elements available as line art, PowerPoint also provides you with an extensive selection of other, more complicated outline shapes to make it easier for you to illustrate your slides in the way that you need. If you click on the AutoShapes button on the <u>Drawing</u> toolbar, the <u>AUTOSHAPES</u> menu will pop up, providing you with a list of eight different sub-menus.

You may need to click on the down-arrows at the bottom of the menu to see the less commonly-used selections. The different options are shown below.

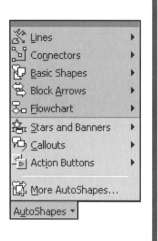

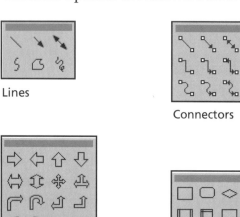

Lines

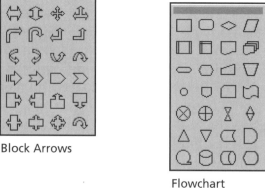

Connectors

Basic Shapes

Block Arrows

Flowchart

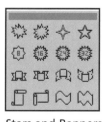

Stars and Banners

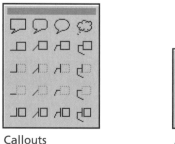

Callouts

Action Buttons

Although most of the AutoShapes are just shapes, some have extra features. The <u>Callout</u> AutoShapes all come with built-in text boxes, so that they can be used as speech bubbles. The <u>Connectors</u> AutoShapes automatically tend to snap to the selection points on other AutoShapes, so as to, well, connect them. The <u>Action Buttons</u> will prompt you to define an Action associated with that shape when you create one – we'll discuss Actions later – but you can click <u>OK</u> without entering one. Finally, the <u>Lines</u> include auto-curved and freehand drawing tools for you to draw your own shapes with. When you bring the line back to its start point, it will finish the object and fill it as appropriate. In addition, text boxes drawn via the <u>Text Box</u> icon can be thought of as rectangular AutoShapes with no default border or fill, that hold text.

Different AutoShapes can be used for different purposes.

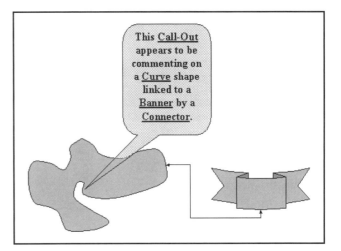

In addition to standard formatting, some AutoShapes have modification handles. When you click on them, in addition to the white selection squares around the shape, you'll see one or more yellow diamonds. Clicking and dragging this diamond modifies the actual shape of the object within its basic style – making a 3-D effect deeper, moving the exact position of a line, changing perspective and so on. If you see a diamond on a selected AutoShape, click and have a play with it to see exactly what it does. You can always <u>Undo</u> the change afterwards.

1 To import a picture to a slide, highlight Picture from the INSERT menu, and then select From File... from the drop Picture sub-menu ...

STATIC DRAWING OBJECTS – PICTURES AND MEDIA CLIPS
There are three types of Drawing Object that cannot be modified via PowerPoint as they are external, but not connected to an editing application. These are pictures, sounds and movie files. They can be inserted into a slide as easily as any other object, moved and resized as required, grouped with other items, and given a border, but that's about it. Media Clips – specifically movie files – have their own AutoLayout placeholders, but the other two do not. They are easy to insert, however.

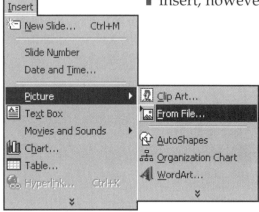

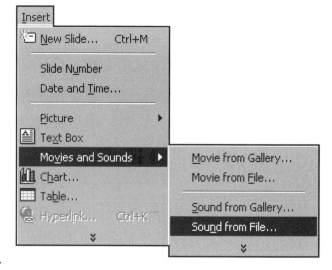

2 ... or to import a Media Clip, highlight Movies and Sounds from the INSERT menu, and then choose either Movie From File... or Sound From File... from the Movies and Sounds sub-menu as appropriate.

3 In each of the three cases, you will get a very similar dialog box titled Insert <Type>. Use this box to locate the file you want to import, and click OK. The static object will be inserted into your slide. Movies will try to display their first frame in the selection box; pictures obviously display the picture; and sounds are represented by a loudspeaker icon.

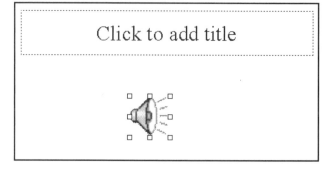

SELECTING OBJECTS

Objects are *selected* when you click on them. This is demonstrated on the screen by square white boxes surrounding the object in question. When these boxes – referred to as handles – are visible, the object can be moved, resized and otherwise formatted and manipulated. Text boxes are slightly more complicated, in that they can also be active – that is, the text inside them is selected, rather than the box itself, and it is the text that can be manipulated rather than the box. The handles are connected by a box outline in both cases – stippled grey when the text box is selected, and slanted lines when active. Non-text items do not have this box.

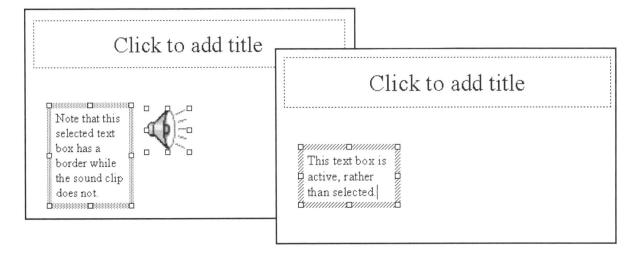

MOVING AND SIZING OBJECTS

At any time, you can click on a handle box and drag it to change the size of an object. Dragging a corner handle and holding <u>Shift</u> down at the same time constrains the object to its current proportions – in other words, if you make it wider, you will make it taller in the same ratio. Some objects are automatically constrained like this whether you hold <u>Shift</u> down or not. If the object is not a text box, you can click on it and drag it to move it around the screen. If it is a text box, however, you need to click on the grey box surrounding it to move it.

OBJECT ORDER

You can add a new Object on top of existing ones at any time, from text boxes and line art through to pictures and movies. In fact, many impressive effects can be obtained by careful manipulation of the order of different objects on your slide – if you add an object the colour of the background over an object that is a different colour, for example, you can give the impression of a carefully-manipulated cutout. The newer the object on the slide, the closer to the top it is… but it will often be desirable to change the order of an object compared to the others on the screen. A selected object can be moved

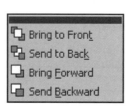

backwards or forwards compared to others, either by one position (Bring Forward or Send Backwards) or all the way (Bring to Front or Send to Back), from the Order sub-menu, accessed via right-clicking the mouse button or from the DRAW menu.

GROUPED OBJECTS

It is possible to lock a set of objects with regards to the way they relate to each other, in terms of position, relative size, ordering and so on – in other words, to make PowerPoint treat them as one object. This is known as grouping. To group two or more objects, they all need to be selected. Once this is the case, you can group the objects by selecting Group from the DRAW menu (an initially hidden item), or by right-clicking, highlighting the Grouping sub-menu from the popup list and clicking on Group. You can remove grouping from a collection of objects with the Ungroup command, located with Group. If you want to experiment, you may be interested to know that many Clip Art images from the Gallery are actually sophisticated groups of AutoShapes, and can be ungrouped once inserted.

THE DRAWING GRID

By default, objects are in PowerPoint are moved and positioned to fit on the lines of an invisible grid made up of 2mm squares. This helps to align everything neatly, and can save a lot of time getting positions exactly right. It is not always entirely convenient, however, and it can be disabled. This option is known as *snapping*, and it is accessed from the DRAW menu. To turn it off, reveal and highlight the Snap option on the DRAW menu, and the Snap submenu will appear.

If the icon next to the To Grid entry is pressed in, click on the entry to disable snapping. You can later click on the same entry to toggle it back on. Toggling snapping on and off does not affect any item until you move it. You can also choose an additional option from the same menu, To Object, which will snap an object you are moving towards the boundaries of other objects on the page. Whether you have snapping on or off, you can manually nudge an object a small distance – smaller than the grid space. You can press the cursor keys to nudge the selected object one space – slightly under 1mm – or you can select the appropriate direction from the initially hidden Nudge submenu of the DRAW menu.

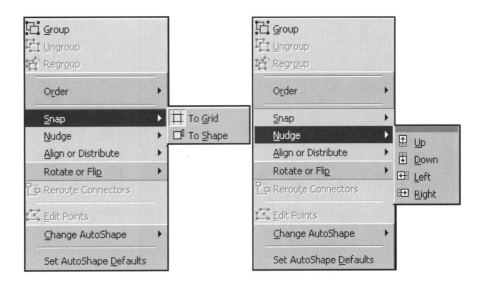

Objects can be aligned using the Snap and Nudge submenus.

FORMATTING OBJECTS

Although the various types of objects are created in different ways, their formatting is carried out in an extremely consistent way. When an object is selected for formatting, the tabs that are available cover all the meaningful options for that particular class of object. An AutoShape with no text box will not provide access to a text formatting tab, for example. Over the next few pages, we'll examine the different formatting options available.

THE FORMATTING DIALOG

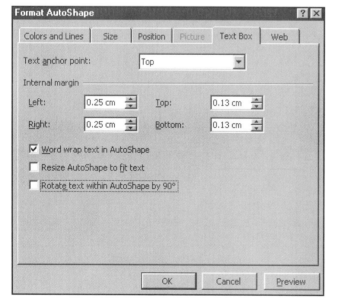

The majority of formatting options can be accessed through the Formatting dialog box. This is obtained in the same way for every item type. The easiest option is to select the item you wish to format and right-click on it. The pop-up menu that appears will include the option Format <TYPE>, such as Format AutoShape or Format Placeholder, depending on what you have selected. You can also select the same option from the FORMAT menu.

You can even rotate your text downwards from this Text formatting tab

BORDERS

Any object, including AutoLayout text and title boxes, can have a border set. This is referred to as a line, and is applied evenly around an entire object. The border options are selected from the third group of icons on the Drawing toolbar. The first icon in the third group, the paint pot, sets the background fill for the Object, which we'll discuss in detail on the next page. The remaining icons, respectively, set options (where available) for Line Color, Font Color, Line Style, Dash Style, Arrow Style, Shadow and 3-D through pop-up selection lists.

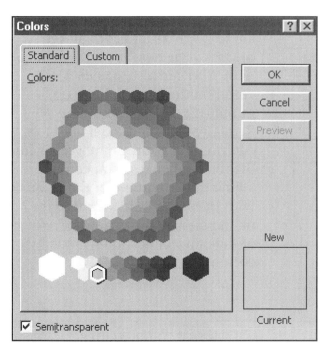

The Fill Color, Line Color and Font Color icons all have small down-arrows to their left and a strip of colour underneath them. These strips show the colour that they are currently set to; selecting an object and clicking on the main icon will apply that colour to that item. Clicking on the arrow to the side will open a colour-picker dialog that displays the colours associated with the current slide scheme. You can click on one to apply it, or select the More Colors option to open a detailed colour-selection palette that you can choose from. You can also access all of these options (apart from the 3-D and Shadow selections) from the Formatting dialog mentioned on the previous page.

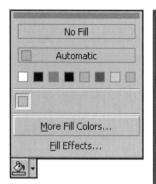

The popup Fill menu.

PLAIN FILLS

Most objects can accept a background fill as part of their formatting. This is accessed from the appropriate formatting dialog, or, more conveniently, from the Fill Color icon on the Drawing toolbar for an object, or selecting Background from the FORMAT toolbar, and then clicking on the colour-picker bar to set the whole slide's background. Whichever method you use to gain access to the fill colour selections, the result looks much the same.

The No Fill and Automatic selection boxes allow you to choose just what they say – no fill at all for the object, or the recommended fill colour for that type of object based on the slide's colour scheme, which we'll discuss shortly. Beneath the Automatic box is a short palette of colours that are associated with – and recommended for – the current slide's design template. You are not restricted to these, however. As mentioned on the previous page, clicking on the More Fill Colors button will bring up the Colors tab, from which one of the 256 standard colours can be selected. If that isn't specific enough though, you can click the Custom tab to get a visual list of all the colours your monitor type can deal with. You can also specify a colour based on the Hue/Saturation/ Luminosity model, or on the Red/Green/Blue model, by entering the appropriate values into the relevant boxes. You can also adjust the brightness of the colour with the slider to the right of the main panel, and preview the effects of the new colour on the slide by clicking Preview.

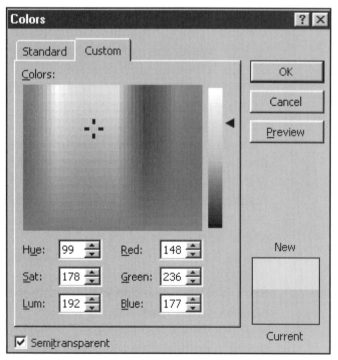

The full range of colours can be selected.

ADVANCED FILLS

In addition to filling a shape with a plain colour, there are four more sophisticated options that are available for you, to help you get precisely the look and feel that you require. They are accessed from the Fill Effects option of the Fill Color pick-list, and each one has its own tab on the Fill Effects dialog.

1 Gradient fills involve a colour ('Color 1') shading to black or white (One-Color mode) or a second colour (Two-Color mode). There are also a number of Preset colours that are more complex.

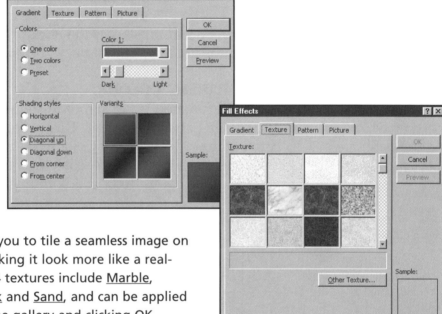

2 Texture fills allow you to tile a seamless image on to your object, making it look more like a real-world item. The 24 textures include Marble, Parchment, Granite, Oak and Sand, and can be applied by selecting one from the gallery and clicking OK.

3 Pattern fills are simple two-colour line patterns that you can apply, such as Dotted Grid and Horizontal Brick. Pick the pattern you want from the palette of 48 and select a foreground and background colour to apply; then click OK.

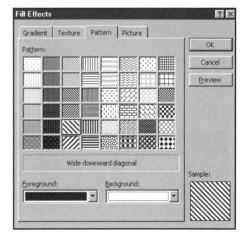

4 Finally, Picture fills let you apply a picture from file to the background of the object. It will be stretched to fit the object without tiling. Click Select Picture, locate and double-click the file you want to use, and click OK.

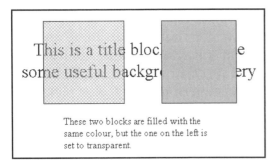

These two blocks are filled with the same colour, but the one on the left is set to transparent.

SEMI-TRANSPARENT FILLS

One option that is often available to you when selecting a plain colour during formatting – particularly for fills and border colours – is to make the item Semi-transparent. This is done through a small tick-box in the bottom left hand corner of the colour palette, visible on both tabs of the Colour Selection dialog. A semi-transparent object is muted in colour intensity, and dimly shows the background it is on top of. Text, unfortunately, cannot be semi-transparent.

TRANSPARENT COLOUR

A related function is the ability to set one colour of an external picture file to be transparent. This is done from the Picture tool-bar via the Set Transparent Color icon, the second from the right. Once the picture is in place, click on the icon, and then click on a patch of the colour to be made transparent in the picture.

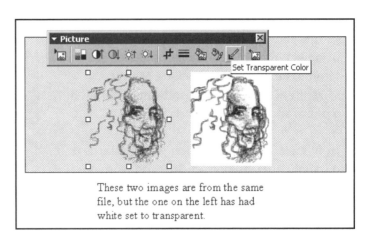

These two images are from the same file, but the one on the left has had white set to transparent.

ALIGNMENT

Objects can be lined up along a common edge or across their centres, or distributed evenly across the slide, by selecting them and choosing the appropriate option from the initially obscured Align or Distribute submenu of the DRAW menu.

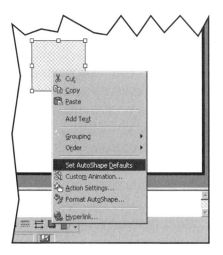

DEFAULTING A STYLE

Several formatting and style selection dialogs include the option to set the currently-selected options in that dialog as the default options for new objects of that type you create. When this option appears as a tick-box, it is labelled <u>Default for New Objects</u>. It also sometimes appears as a menu item, in which case it reads Set <TYPE> Default. Once you select this option, the style you choose will remain in place as the default option until you set a new default. Applying a design template will over-ride your preset defaults, but only temporarily.

COLOUR SCHEMES

Each slide has a colour scheme. This is a restricted palette of colours that will be used, by default, for the colours of the various objects, lines and pieces of text. You may set a different slide colour scheme for each slide, or apply it to the whole presentation, and it will override your current defaults. You can choose from a selection of standard schemes, or create an entirely new custom scheme and apply it, add it to the standard schemes, or both. You may have up to 16 standard schemes at one time. The <u>Color Scheme</u> dialog is accessed through the <u>Slide Color Schemes...</u> option of the <u>FORMAT</u> menu.

You can personalize your slide <u>Color Scheme</u>.

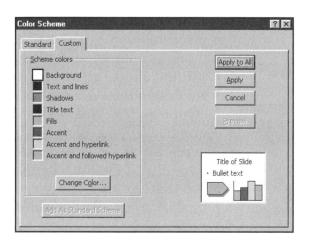

The Master Slide (shown above) sets the style defaults and backgrounds for slides in the presentation (shown below).

MASTER SLIDES

Occasionally, you will want to have an item appearing on every slide in a presentation, to apply a consistent default format for your titles, or otherwise modify the basic pattern of your presentation. This is done through the Master slides. A Master slide provides the Slide AutoLayout system with the exact positions for its placeholders, and also defines different text styles and formats for slide titles, AutoLayout text boxes and placeholders. In addition, any object added to a Master slide will be displayed in the deepest layer of the background for all the slides based on the Master. The Master Slides are accessed from the Master submenu of the VIEW menu. Initially, only the Slide Master is visible; the Title Master, Notes Master and Handout Master can be accessed by clicking on the down-arrows at the bottom of the sub-menu. You can click on a View icon (or select a view from the VIEW menu) to exit a Master Slide, or click Close on the floating toolbar.

SUPPRESSING MASTER INFO

Although the formatting applied to the Master Slide placeholders will always be applied to every slide by default – it can, of course, be changed, but PowerPoint needs to have *some* positional info and text styles to apply to headings and AutoLayouts – you can choose to suppress display of any extra objects added to the Master Slide as background graphics. If you select Background from the FORMAT menu, you'll see a box at the bottom of the slide Background dialog box entitled Omit background graphics from master. If you tick this box and Apply it, Objects on the Master slide will not be shown. This option can also be applied to the entire presentation by clicking Apply to All, if you so wish.

The <u>Title Master</u> (above) and <u>Slide Master</u> (below) from the Network Blitz template.

THE TITLE MASTER

The <u>Title Master</u> slide sets the appearance and patterns of slides created with the Title Slide AutoLayout. It has no effect on any of the other slides. As with all Master slides, items can be added to display in the background, and the Title and Subtitle placeholders will accept all the usual range of font formatting and can themselves be moved, resized and formatted – filled, bordered and so on. One interesting point to note is that in some installations of PowerPoint 2000, the <u>Title Master</u> option is deactivated for some blank presentations. If you find you have this trouble and need access to the <u>Title Master</u>, start with a design template. You can then access the <u>Title Master</u> (and the other Masters) and delete the template's graphics before setting your own styles.

THE SLIDE MASTER

The <u>Slide Master</u> is used for all new slides other than the Title Slide AutoLayout. It works in exactly the same way as the Title Master. The main points of difference are the size of the AutoLayout area box, within which all AutoLayout items are placed, and the bullet list placeholders. Bullet list items can be <u>Promoted</u> and <u>Demoted</u> – full details are available later in the book – but this affects their position on screen, formatting and entire general impact. Demoted bullets are used for making important sub-points. The <u>Second</u>, <u>Third</u>, <u>Fourth</u> and <u>Fifth</u> level bullet formats on the Slide Master are used to control the formatting of the various levels of demotion that the bullets can go through.

PLACEHOLDER TEXT AND TEXT BOXES

It is worth taking a moment to mention that changing the actual text displayed in a Master Slide placeholder has no effect. That text is not used; it is merely there to tell you what that part of the Master Slide is used for. The text of the 'Click Here to add <Type>' messages you see on incomplete AutoLayout Slides is generated automatically. If you want to add text to a Master Slide you will need to draw a text box on the Master, type the text you want into it and format it as you require. This text will, of course, appear on every relevant slide, exactly as you have formatted it, in the same position.

THE NOTES MASTER AND HANDOUT MASTER

The remaining two Master Slides allow you to format and otherwise modify any notes pages and handouts that you may want to access or print. They are used much less than the Title and Slide Masters, and it may be that you never require them at all. However, they are there for you to make use of if required. You can change the sizes and positions of the Slide box and the Text box on the <u>Notes Master</u>, but you cannot change the size, shape, position or number of the slide placeholders on the <u>Handout Master</u>.

The <u>Handouts Master</u> (right) and <u>Notes Master</u> (far right) allow you to set general formats for your notes and handouts.

FINISHING TOUCHES

5

Once you have your presentation the way you want it, there are some other things you may want to take into consideration before printing it. It is always worth making sure that your spelling is correct; nothing looks more amateurish than glaring spelling mistakes and typographical errors. You might also want to run your presentation as an on-screen slideshow, to make sure that all your slides look correct. Finally, you will need to know how to go about printing out the different parts of your presentations.

POLISHING YOUR TEXT

Effective display and design is just one part of making sure your text is effective. It also has to grab the reader, and that means making sure it is spelled correctly. Typographical errors – known as typos – immediately alienate your readers. The error calls all your work into question. It is therefore worth taking some time to check for mistakes.

AUTOMATIC SPELL-CHECKING

Right-click on a spelling error to select from a list of corrections.

We all make typos. Even a professional writer will hit the wrong key one time in 30 on average, and as many as 10 per cent of those errors may slip by without being immediately noticed. Luckily, PowerPoint keeps track of immediate mistakes for you. While you work, the program checks the text you type behind the scenes for you. When it finds a word that it does not recognise, that word is underlined with a wavy red line, indicating an error. If you right-click on the word, the menu that pops up will start with a list of correctly-spelled words that PowerPoint thinks you might have wanted. Click on one to apply it as a correction.

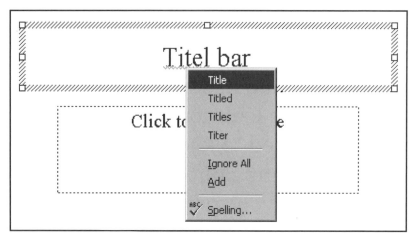

ALTERNATIVE OPTIONS

You don't have to correct the word, if you are sure it is spelled correctly. One option is always just to ignore the red line. They can get distracting however, so a second option is to select Ignore All from the pop-up menu. This will tell PowerPoint that, for this particular session – in other words, until the program is shut down – it is to treat all instances of that word as if they were known to be correct. If you are certain that the word is correct – a company name, for example – you can teach the word to PowerPoint by clicking Add. This will store the word in a special dictionary of added words, called a custom dictionary, so that it is always remembered.

AUTOCORRECT

Some words will be automatically corrected without you having to do anything. PowerPoint has a list of approximately 1,200 of the most common typing mistakes, such as **thsi** instead of **this**, or **knwo** instead of **know**. If it spots one of the words on its list, it will replace it with the correct word automatically. It also capitalises the names of days and the initial letters of sentences, corrects the second capital of a word with two **INitial CApitals** and corrects accidental activation of the Caps Lock key. This is known as AutoCorrect.

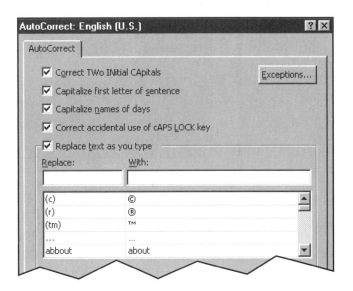

The AutoCorrect dialog box allows you to specify which common errors are automatically corrected.

AUTOCORRECT OPTIONS

The list of words used by the AutoCorrect function can be examined, added to or deleted from the <u>AutoCorrect dialog box</u>, obtained by selecting <u>AutoCorrect</u> from the <u>TOOLS</u> menu. You can deactivate the various options – <u>Correct Two Initial Capitals</u>, <u>Capitalize first letter of sentence</u>, <u>Capitalize names of days</u>, <u>Correct accidental use of caps lock key</u> and the main option, <u>Replace text as you type</u>, by unticking their respective boxes, but this is not really recommended. You can add a new AutoCorrect option by inserting the wrong and right forms into the top text boxes and clicking <u>Add</u>, and you can delete an entry by highlighting it and clicking <u>Delete</u>.

MANUAL SPELL-CHECKING

If you do not want to deal with spelling errors as they arise, you can tell PowerPoint to perform a full check of all the spelling in a document by pressing <u>F7</u> on the keyboard, selecting <u>Spelling...</u> from the <u>TOOLS</u> menu, or clicking on the tick-shaped <u>Spelling</u> icon on the main toolbar.

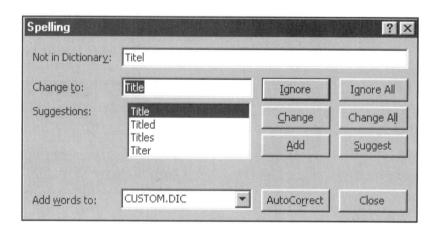

When you perform a check, as soon as PowerPoint finds a word it does not recognize it will show you the dialog box above. From this box, you can ignore that particular occasion of the word (or all occasions of it) by clicking <u>Ignore</u> or <u>Ignore All</u>, you can replace just the current instance of the word (or

all of them) with the currently-highlighted selection from the
Change To box by clicking Change or Change All, teach
PowerPoint the word by clicking Add or add the spelling
error and its correction to the AutoCorrect system by clicking
the AutoCorrect button.

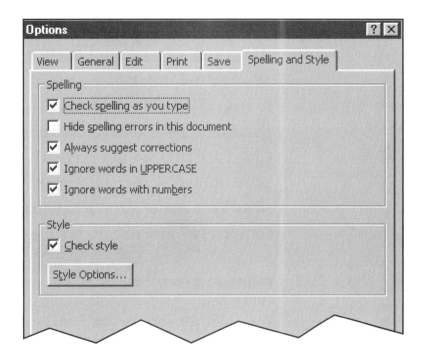

FURTHER OPTIONS

A selection of other optional modifications to the spell-
checking system is available from the Spelling and Style tab of
the Options dialog box, accessed through the TOOLS menu.
You can disable the background spell-checking system by
deselecting the Check spelling as you type option, or hide the
evidence of the background spell-checking by selecting Hide
spelling errors in this document. If you deselect Always
suggest corrections, incorrect words will be identified, but the
system will not provide you with a list of possible correct
words. You can also exempt uppercase words and words that
contain numbers by ticking the appropriate Ignore... box.
Select the options you want and click OK.

PRINTING YOUR PRESENTATION

Almost all presentations will need to be printed out at some point or other, even if it is just to allow you to have a good look at your slides. On-screen slides that are to be converted to transparencies or 35mm slides are printed in exactly the same way as if the presentation was to be printed on to paper. The first stage is to make sure that your work is as correct and complete as possible, to help save you time and money.

FINAL CHECKS

When you're getting ready to print out your presentation – particularly if you are going to print it on to a transparency or 35mm slide – you need to make sure you minimize the

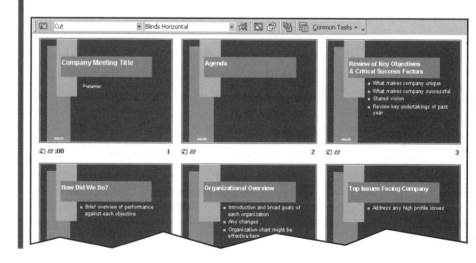

Slide Sorter View gives you a clear overview of your presentation.

number of errors that remain in your document. If you have created a document it can be very difficult to notice mistakes, because your mind is already familiar with them and tries to skip over them. The first step, therefore, is to read over all the text in your presentation slowly and carefully. Don't worry about the formatting at this point; just check for spelling, grammar and accuracy. Although the spell-check functions are extremely powerful, they cannot spot typos that are valid words in their own right – "two much" instead of "too much", for example. You may want to set the display to <u>Black and White</u>, (accessed from the <u>VIEW</u> menu as discussed earlier), for this read-through, as it will offer fewer distractions.

RUNNING A SLIDE SHOW

Once you're happy with the way that the text in your presentation reads, you should spend some time looking at the layout and design elements for consistency. It can be surprisingly easy to miss a design error between different slides – clashing backgrounds, subtle differences in font and style and so on, that makes all the difference between a good presentation and a stunning one. The best way to check the design is to run a standard on-screen Slide Show and check the slides in context with one another. Press <u>F5</u> on your keyboard or select <u>View Show</u> from the <u>SLIDE SHOW</u> menu to start the show. Each slide will be displayed full-size on your screen; to move to the next slide in the show, click the left mouse button. As each slide comes up, examine it closely for errors or flaws. The show will end when there are no more slides to display, or you can press <u>Esc</u> to stop the show early. Slide Shows get a lot more powerful than this basic form, and are discussed fully in the next chapter.

This is a slideshow!

Note the absence of toolbars or menus...

PRINTING

When you are ready to print your document, select <u>Print...</u> from the <u>File</u> menu. The <u>Print</u> dialog box will appear:

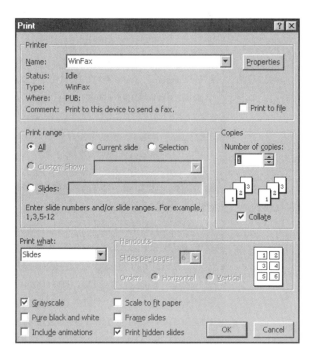

The <u>Print Range</u> area of the dialog tells the printer which slides to print from your presentation. To print a sub-section, click on <u>Slides</u> and then enter the range of pages to print. The <u>Print what</u> area defines the specific items that you will be printing – either the <u>Slides</u>, the presentation <u>Outline</u>, the speaker's <u>Notes</u> pages for each slide or <u>Handouts</u>, slide miniatures. In the <u>Copies</u> area, you can define how many copies of your slides PowerPoint will print – just alter the number in the <u>Number of copies</u> box. If <u>Collate</u> is ticked, copies will be printed as entire sets of the document, one after another; if it is unticked, each page will print all its copies before moving on to the next page. The image above the <u>Collate</u> box demonstrates this. The <u>Printer</u> area of the <u>Print</u> dialog is fairly advanced, so only modify it if you know what you are doing.

PRINT OPTIONS

There are several other aspects of the print process that you can modify to suit your needs better. The Handouts area of the print dialog is activated when you select Handouts from the Print what drop-down pick list. You can then choose the layout that the slide images are printed in on the Handouts pages. Clicking on the Slides per page box opens a dropdown list from which you can choose standard layouts of either 2, 3, 4, 6 or 9 slides to be printed per page. The preview icon to the right of the Handouts area displays the new layout. You can also choose whether the slides are ordered across the page (Horizontal), or down it (Vertical).

A block of options towards the bottom left of the print dialog allows you to control the way that slides are displayed by the print process. You can select the Greyscale or Pure black-and-white tick-boxes to have PowerPoint convert the slides for non-colour printers, although the printer itself will probably do a good job too if necessary. Selecting Pure black-and-white prints slides the way they appear when the Black-and-white option is selected from the VIEW menu. Scale to fit paper forces PowerPoint to resize your presentation to match the printer's full paper size – which can look very odd if your slides are a radically different size or layout to your paper.

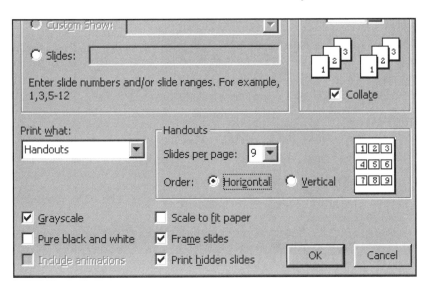

The Handouts section of the Print dialog is used to set options for printing slide miniatures.

SOME DESIGN TIPS

There are a few useful things to bear in mind when preparing an attractive, effective presentation. Most of these are already incorporated into the design templates, but you may prefer to create your own designs – the various PowerPoint default options do become familiar to people who attend a lot of presentations, or who work with PowerPoint themselves. We'll include some images for you to show examples of what you *shouldn't* be doing!

Don't use lots of different fonts – it looks messy and jumbled. Try to stick to two or three as a maximum – ideally just one for titles and one for body text.

ⓇËVẼÑÜË *and* Profit

- **This** IS a most **unfair** DISTORTION **OF** the COMPANY MEETING presentation!
- FORECAST VS ACTUAL
- *Gross Margin*
- **IMPORTANT** trends
- COMPARE company
- Use MULTIPLE SLIDES to break out MEANINGFUL DETAIL

Text formatting can be a very useful way of bringing attention to certain words, but only if it stands out by being uncommon. Use bold, italic and underline, but sparingly.

Think about the purpose that your document is to serve. If you are preparing data for a formal report, stick to a serious serif font and do not add lots of bright colours, tints, shades or cheerful formatting.

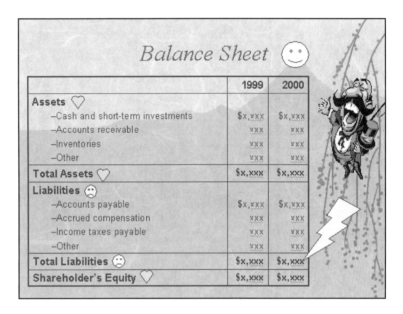

A background tint to text boxes that hold important information – titles, totals and so on – can really make them stand out. Make sure the background doesn't overwhelm the text, though.

Colour can be a great way of drawing attention but, like text formatting, it works best when used sparingly. You can also use colour to categorize different types of information.

A title centred across the page reads more like a headline. Sometimes this can be useful. You will rarely want to use centred text for bullet lists though, they look scrappy that way.

Remember to include page numbers for long presentations. Most of all, though, make the work easy to look at. If it is eye-bending or difficult to read people will simply not bother, and your work will be wasted.

Stick to a consistent style. Different styles on different slides will look somewhat hysterical, and may confuse the message that you are trying to convey.

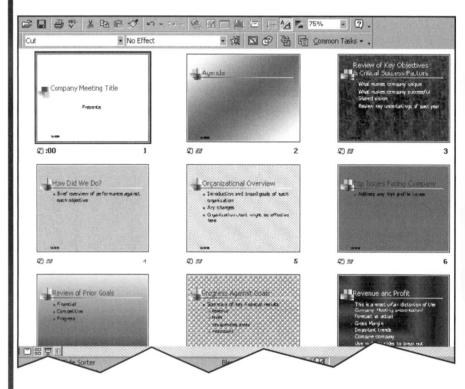

If you apply a design template or other major stylistic change, always make sure that you go back over every slide afterwards because AutoLayout placeholders may be moved, and that might throw out your designs.

If you need to build a complex graphic or background that you're having trouble with, it may be more effective to create it in an image manipulation program such as Freehand or PageMaker, and then import it as a solid picture.

BASIC SLIDE SHOWS

6

Much of the time, getting your slides finished is only one part of the job – because the slides still have to be presented. If you're planning to hold a meeting or give a talk, you're going to need to arrange your presentation correctly and make sure you've got a complete set of notes so you're not lost for words. Even if your document is destined for a solely electronic life it may still be viewed as a Slide Show, and speaker's notes can be used as extended footnotes if the file is going to be distributed.

INTRODUCTION TO PRESENTATIONS

PowerPoint is geared up to providing you with all the possible tools that you might want in order to use its presentations as on-screen Slide Shows. With that in mind, it's worth considering using a computer projection of a PowerPoint Slide Show for any talk or meeting you need to give. We'll look at the basics of Slide Shows over the next few pages, and explore the advanced functions later, in the next chapter.

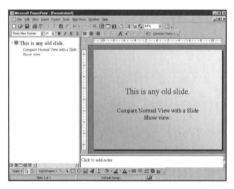

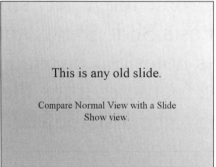

WHAT EXACTLY IS A SLIDE SHOW?

A PowerPoint presentation, as we have previously discussed, is made up of a series of slides. Each slide generally contains a fairly restricted amount of information presented in a clear, accessible, visually attractive style. In the most basic type of Slide Show, the slides in your presentation are displayed one after another in a rolling sequence in the order that they appear in your document. Each slide is shown full-screen, with no toolbars, dialog boxes, labels or any other foreign material. When the mouse is clicked, the current slide is replaced by the one after it in the presentation. After the last slide has been shown, the Slide Show ends.

WHAT IS A SLIDE SHOW USED FOR?

The most obvious purpose of a PowerPoint Slide Show is to provide an electronic version of a real, physical slide show – in other words, to support a speech, presentation or other talk hosted by a speaker. In the physical sense, a slide show is used to provide visual support to a speech, to identify key items and points for the audience to focus on, to summarise information, to allow for visual backup to help prove or illustrate specific points and to demonstrate trends or results. PowerPoint Slide Shows can and will do all of these things for you, and make an invaluable addition to any public speaking that you may have to do. There are other purposes which a Slide Show can be used for, though. As you'll discover later,

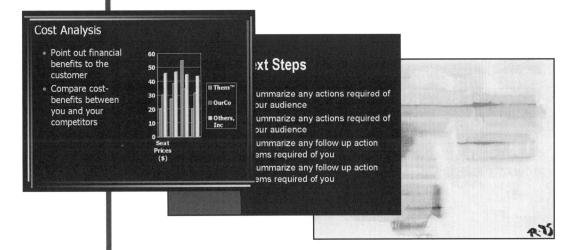

Slide Shows can be navigated through the use of special action buttons that function as hyperlinks, and that can be used to jump to other slides, even to other presentations. That means that you can use a Slide Show or a set of Slide Shows as an form of off-line website, or as a general format for distributing other forms of structured data. You can also make the presentation run automatically, even adding recorded narration, so that you can use the Slide Show even when there is noone there at all, as a form of mini-movie, which can work very well as a rolling demo at an unmanned booth or stand. You can even convert your Slide Show to a web site.

RUNNING YOUR PRESENTATION AS A SLIDE SHOW

The actual logistics of running the most basic form of Slide Show are very simple, and you can do it at any time.

1 From the <u>SLIDE SHOW</u> menu, select the <u>View Show</u> option. You can also press <u>F5</u> on the keyboard, if you prefer.

2 Your screen will be given over completely to the Slide Show. Each slide will be displayed full-screen, holding just the elements that you have placed on it or otherwise selected.

3 To move to the next slide in the show, click on the left mouse button. When the Show ends – when there are no more slides to show, or when you press the Esc button on your keyboard – you are returned to your previous view.

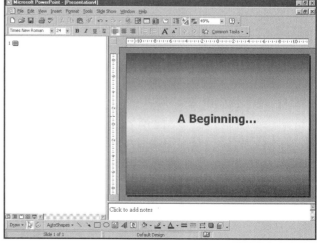

SLIDE TIMING

You don't have to have each – or, indeed, any – slide in your Slide Show pause until you click the mouse button. You can also assign a time to a slide, after which the show will move on.

1 Switch to <u>Slide Sorter</u> view and click once on a slide that you want to set a time limit for, selecting it. Then select <u>Slide Transition</u> from the <u>SLIDE SHOW</u> menu, or click on the <u>Slide Transition</u> icon, the leftmost one on the Slide Sorter tool bar that is shown in Slide Sorter view below the standard and formatting toolbars.

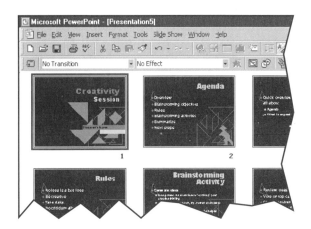

2 The <u>Slide Transition</u> dialog box will appear. Don't worry about most of it for the moment. In the bottom left corner is an area called <u>Advance</u>. Tick the <u>Automatically after</u> box, and either enter a time as Minutes:Seconds over the default of 00:00 that appears, or use the up and down arrows to set a time.

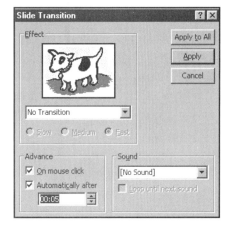

3 To apply this timed advance to the current slide, click <u>Apply</u>. To apply it to the entire presentation, click <u>Apply to All.</u> Your timing will be set, and the slide/s will now advance automatically as you have chosen. The new timing will be displayed in the Slide Sorter view as a time figure under the bottom left corner of the slide.

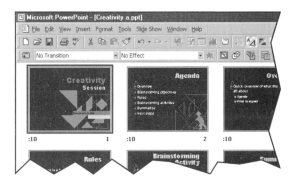

DISPLAY POINTERS

Although by default the mouse pointer is not shown during a presentation, it is possible to display it, if you need to indicate a certain area or object. If you move the mouse slightly during a presentation, nothing will appear to happen. If you move it around smoothly for a second or two however, the mouse pointer will automatically be displayed. From that time on, you can move the pointer around the screen as normal, and use it to highlight or display items as required. You can also press <u>Ctrl-A</u> to display the arrow pointer. When you want to hide it again, you can press <u>Ctrl-H</u> to get rid of it.

There is another option available to you, and that is to use the pointer as a pen to temporarily annotate the slide. Pressing <u>Ctrl-P</u> will show the pointer, if it is hidden, and make it look like a pen. When it is in this form, you can use the mouse as a pen on the slide, clicking on the left mouse button to leave a black line. You can use this simple drawing tool to circle important information, underline key points for emphasis, and so on. Pressing <u>Ctrl-A</u> or <u>Esc</u> will turn the pen pointer back into an arrow again, at which point you will be able to left-click to move to the next slide, or <u>Esc</u> to end. Any annotation you draw on to the slide will be lost as soon as the next slide is opened or the show is ended.

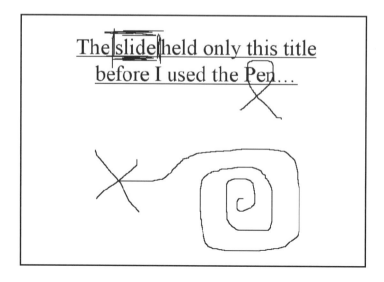

The <u>Slide Options</u> shortcut menu accessed during slide shows.

SLIDE OPTIONS

There are a number of options you can select while a Slide Show is active. Right-clicking the mouse button brings up a <u>Slide Options</u> popup menu, from which you can select specific slides to jump to, format the pointer – including the colour of the pen's trail – access Speakers Notes or the Meeting Minder, turn the screen black or pause animations.

When the pop-up menu is active, the Slide Show will be put on hold temporarily while you make your selections. <u>Next</u> and <u>Previous</u> will move you forwards or backwards in the Slide Show respectively. <u>Go</u> will allow you to open the <u>Slide Navigator</u> dialog, or to select a slide to jump to by its title. Meeting Minder will be covered later, but Speaker Notes shows you the notes for that slide.

<u>Pointer Options</u> lets you choose whether to treat the pointer as normally hidden by default (<u>Automatic</u>), totally hidden no matter what mouse moves you make (<u>Hidden</u>), as an arrow (<u>Arrow</u>) or as an annotation tool (<u>Pen</u>), and the <u>Pen Colour</u> option lets you pick a colour for the lines you draw – useful if a slide is very dark, as the default pen colour is black.

<u>Screen</u> allows you to pause on-screen animations, set the screen to black rather than the default white, or to erase Pen annotations. Finally, you can access the automatic Help functions, or click on <u>End Show</u> to return to PowerPoint.

The <u>Slide Navigator</u> and <u>Pointer Options</u> are accessed through the <u>Slide Options</u> shortcut menu.

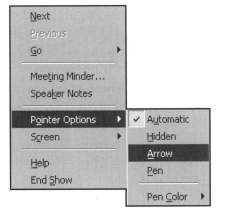

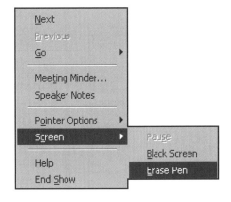

MANIPULATING SLIDES

You can do almost as much with a completed slide as you can do to its contents. When you work with your presentation as a whole rather than concentrating on getting the individual elements correct – separating the various stages of producing a full show is always sensible – you may well find that there are certain changes that you need to make to your slides in terms of their contribution to the presentation, rather than in terms of their contents or design.

The Slide Outline view in either Expanded mode (above) or Collapsed mode (below) remains a powerful tool.

SLIDE OUTLINE DETAILS

The Slide Outline provides you with editorial access to text generated through the AutoLayouts, as mentioned earlier. Titles, Subtitles and Text from the Slide AutoLayout system are all shown in full on the Slide Outline, and you can access that text from there too – it's not just for display. This is often extremely convenient, and it is a powerful feature. However, it can also be risky. If you want to work with slides in the Outline you may find that, rather than whole slides, you accidentally work with their components. This can lead to confusion and introduce errors, so sometimes it is useful to turn it off. To deactivate Slide Outline details, click in the Outline window and then choose Select All from the EDIT menu. With the whole Outline selected, right-click in the Outline window and select Collapse from the pop-up menu. All slide details will be obscured. To reveal them again, Select All the Outline, right-click on it and select Expand.

FORMATTING DETAILS

Another Outline option, if you want to get a clearer image of your slide contents without going over the slides one by one, is to enable the Outline to show slide formatting details. Once again, this applies only to the AutoLayout text on the slides – remember that the text inside drawing objects, which includes manually-drawn text boxes, is not recognized by the Outline. Using the default settings, enabling formatting details is fairly straightforward.

1 Click on the More Buttons icon on the main toolbar – the right arrows in the centre of the merged icon bar.

2 A small pop-up palette of icons will appear below the right arrows. The Show Formatting icon is located within that palette.

3 Click on this icon to switch on the text formatting display in the Outline. While this is active, text in the Outline will be displayed as closely to the main text as possible, though do remember that the magnification of the Outline window is usually less than that of the Slide window, so it will be smaller.

4 If you want to deactivate the formatting display again, you will find that the icon has moved to the main toolbar, next to the Zoom box, as part of PowerPoint's passive customisation system. Click the icon again to turn the formatting display off.

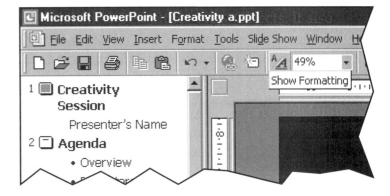

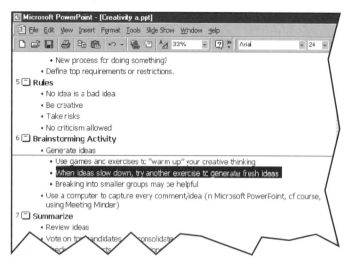

MOVING TEXT

The Outline view gives you access to a number of convenient options for dragging and dropping individual text items between slides. You can move bullet points around within a slide or from one slide to another, and you can move titles around just as easily too. To move a bullet point, subtitle or non-bulleted paragraph of text, move the mouse pointer just to the left of the bullet (or the start of text if the paragraph is not bulleted).

When it turns into an arrowed cross, you can click and drag to move the text as one unit. The new position that the text will occupy is indicated by a thin black line. If you drop unbulleted text into a bullet list, it will become bulleted to fit in with the information around it, and vice versa.

Individual sections of text can be manipulated in a similar manner. Rather than selecting the whole slide as described above, you can click and drag or double-click within the text to select some or all of it, then click on the text and drag it to its new position. The insertion point displayed is a standard drag-and-drop insertion cursor. As before, the text you move will take on the default properties of the type of placeholder box that it is being inserted into. Title text can be moved in or out using the same method.

PROMOTION AND DEMOTION

Text held in AutoLayout placeholders is considered by the program to have a rank, used to calculate the level of bullet style applied from the Master slides. There are five ranks of paragraph text. The default rank is rank 1, the highest text rank. Subheading text is also considered to be rank 1, and unless the Title Master defines otherwise, it is based on a rank 1 bullet, just without actually being part of a bullet list. By default, ranks 2 to 5 get progressively smaller, and are

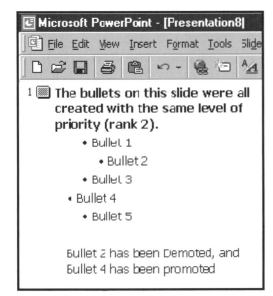

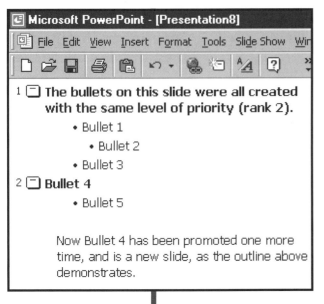

indented further and further to the right. This is used to indicate priority in a bullet list. Title text counts as one rank more important than rank 1, so could be considered as rank 0. You can promote text up a rank by clicking on it and then selecting the <u>Promote</u> icon, a thick green arrow pointing to the left that can initially be found within the <u>More Buttons</u> box of the <u>Formatting</u> menu – the right arrows at the far right of the toolbar in the default set-up. You can similarly demote it by clicking the Demote icon next to it, a thick green right arrow. You can also demote by clicking in the item on the outline and pressing <u>Tab</u>, or promote by pressing <u>Shift-Tab</u>.

If you clicked on the text in the Outline view, you can go one stage further and promote a rank 1 bullet to a title, or demote a title to a rank 1 bullet. A promotion of this sort creates a new slide based on the Bulleted List AutoLayout. The title of the new slide will be the promoted list item, and its contents will consist of any design template and/or Master material plus, as a bulleted list, any remaining AutoLayout text between the newly promoted list item and the end of the slide it was on. Similarly, demoting a title will attach it, and all the items that follow it, as bullet items on the slide above it. The slide it titled will be lost, with Drawing objects and non-AutoLayout text added to the slide simply discarded – so do take care.

MOVING SLIDES

The most effective method of moving slides, much like moving body text, is to use drag-and-drop within the Slide Outline section. When you move the mouse pointer over an Outline icon depicting a slide, it turns into the cross discussed earlier. Click on that slide icon, and the entire slide will be selected. This will be represented in the outline by the slide icon, title and all its contents being selected. You can then drag-and-drop the slide to move it to a new position within the presentation. Note that the entire slide is moved, not just its outline text, so drawing objects and text boxes will be moved too. If you drop the slide into the middle of a list or set of paragraphs in the outline, then the list items that appear below the slide's new position are added to the bottom of the slide that was moved as extra bullet points.

You can move an entire slide by selecting and dragging in the Outline.

It is also worth noting at this point that if you move the text insertion cursor to the end of a slide's title in the Outline view and press Return, a new slide with a blank title will appear immediately after the old slide's title in the Outline. This new slide comes between the old slide's title and its bullets. The text on the old slide will be moved to the new slide, but not the Drawing Objects. Similarly, moving the insertion point to the start of the title and pressing Backspace will act as if you demoted the title, deleting the current slide and attaching its title and Outline bullets to the previous slide as additional bullets.

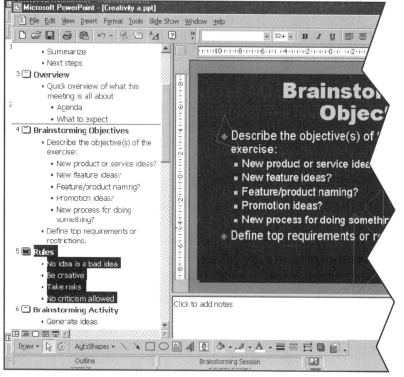

DUPLICATING SLIDES

The quick way of duplicating a slide is using <u>Copy</u> and <u>Paste</u>.

1 In the outline view, select the entire slide by clicking on the <u>Slide Icon</u> between the slide's number and its title.

2 Select <u>Copy</u> from the <u>EDIT</u> menu, or press Ctrl-C.

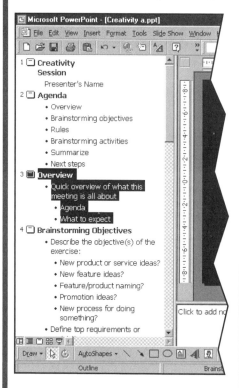

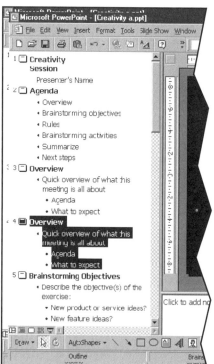

3 Move the cursor to a point in the outline in the slide before the space you want to insert the copied slide into – i.e. if you want to create the new slide between slides 1 and 2, you would click on a point in slide 1. Select <u>Paste</u> from the <u>EDIT</u> menu or press <u>Ctrl-V</u> to paste the new slide into position.

Alternatively, you can click somewhere in the <u>Outline</u> for the slide you want to copy, and select <u>Duplicate Slide</u> from the <u>INSERT</u> menu. This will copy the slide and place it immediately after the original. You can then click and drag on the new slide to move it into the position you want.

NOTES AND COMMENTS

You can add a lot of subsidiary information to a slide – material that will be accessible from an electronic copy of the file, but that does not get displayed in a Slide Show or printed up on to transparencies. Over the next few pages we'll have a look at two of the more important forms of subsidiary material, Speakers Notes and Slide Comments.

SPEAKERS NOTES

Notes are a form of text-based information that is associated with a slide, but is not actually displayed with it or printed with it. They're mostly used, as the name suggests, to provide you with space to work out in detail what you're going to actually say for each slide when you present it, so that you don't have to rely on the slide itself to jog your memory. A slide, remember, should just summarise the most salient points of one section of a speech. Adding Speakers Notes is simplicity itself; you just click in the Notes section directly below the slide, and type. You may find it more convenient to enter notes from <u>Outline View</u> by clicking on the <u>Outline View</u> icon in the bottom left of the screen. Notes can accept all the usual types of basic text formatting, including fonts, point size, styles, colours and so on.

The <u>Outline View</u> icon.

VIEWING NOTES

You can examine the Notes pages that PowerPoint automatically generates from the material you've entered using the Notes View. This shows you how the Speakers Notes are going to look once they're printed out on paper. This view is based on the Notes Master template (pictured left) and assigns one page to each slide, with the slide printed at roughly half-size in the top half of the page and the notes themselves printed below it. You can also edit Notes text in this view. To get access to this screen, select Notes Page from the VIEW menu. There is

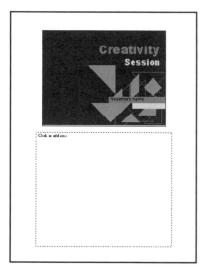

no default Notes Page View icon, so you'll have to do it manually.

If you want to change the default set-up for the Notes Pages, you'll need to make changes in the Notes Master. Click and resize or drag the Master placeholders for the Slide area and the Notes area in order to get the Notes Pages more to your liking.

PRINTING NOTES

To print the Speaker's Notes, Select Print... from the FILE menu. When the Print dialog comes up, select Notes Pages from the Print what dropdown pick list. Assuming that your printer is set up correctly, you can then just click on the OK button to print your notes.

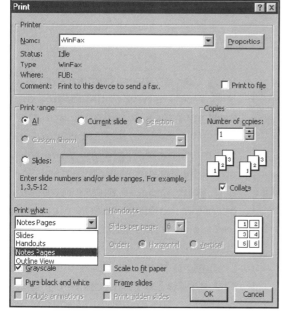

SLIDE COMMENTS

Comments are like sticky reminder notes – small, pale yellow text-boxes that you can add on top of a slide to make an observation or comment, or remind yourself of things left to do, particularly when associated with the slide in question. They are generally used to allow people to review a presentation and make suggestions/ask questions about material on slides in a way that can be easily identified but is not permanent. Comments do appear on a Slide Show or print-out of the slide when activated, but can be turned on and off with a simple command. When they are turned off, which is their default setting, there are not displayed, either on the screen, on a Slide Show or on a print-out.

1 To activate Slide Comments, select Comments from the VIEW menu. The first time you use the button, it will be hidden.

2 The Reviewing tool bar will appear beneath your usual toolbars. The first five icons of this bar allow you to Insert Comment, Show/Hide Comments, select the Previous Comment or the Next Comment or to Delete Comment.

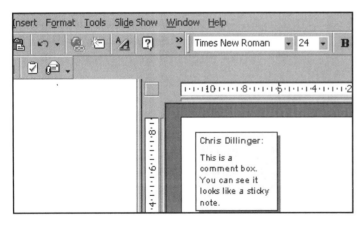

3 Click on Insert Comment to create a new comment box on your slide. It will appear in the top left corner or, if there is already a comment there, slightly in from that point. By default, new comments start with your name, so that other people participating in the review process can see who said what. To hide comments again, you can select Comments from the VIEW menu or click on the Show/Hide Comments button on the Reviewing toolbar.

ADVANCED SHOWS

7

In the previous chapter, we discussed how to set up and run a basic Slide Show. You don't have to restrict yourself to static slides, though. PowerPoint provides a number of powerful tools to help you bring your Slide Shows to life. In the next chapter, we'll look at the different ways that you can enhance your Slide Shows, from animating the appearance of each object on your slides through to special transitionary cuts and fades between the slides themselves. We'll also look at ways you can link between slides; even to other presentations.

SLIDE ANIMATIONS

There are a number of ways that you can add some life to your presentations with the aid of PowerPoint's built-in functions. One of the simplest and most effective involves using slide animations, a wide selection of pre-prepared special effects for introducing an item to your slide. In this section we'll have a look at the various animations that are available, and how to apply them to your slides' objects.

This title is not animated

This subtitle is Dissolving onto the screen.

INTRODUCTION TO ANIMATIONS

Slide animations are special ways of introducing an object on to your slide. They take effect during slide shows: when the slide appears, objects without animations appear with it. Then the various animated objects are introduced one by one, in an order and a timing of your choosing, according to the animations set for them. You can select the relative order by which animated objects are introduced, and every object on the slide, from the title down to an imported OLE object, can carry an animation. This gives you complete flexibility over the way that your slide's items appear on the screen.

1 From the SLIDE SHOW menu, select Custom Animation. The Custom Animation dialog box will appear. Note that this dialog allows you to modify the animations for just the current slide's objects.

ANIMATING OBJECTS

There are two ways to animate an object. If you just want to add animation to a small selection of the objects on your slide – say one or two – then the quickest way to do so is going to be to click on the object, highlight the Preset Animation option from the SLIDE SHOW menu and pick one of the animation types. This will apply the animation according to the Slide Show's default settings, and if you animate more than one object they will be handled in the order in which they are layered on the page, from the rearmost forward. The alternative, however, is more powerful.

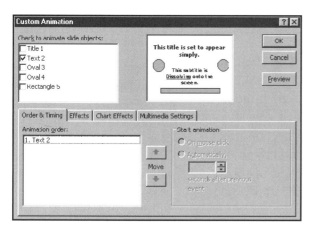

2 Tick the boxes to the left of the objects you want to animate in the Check to animate slide list. All objects on the slide are listed here, by type, in the order that they are layered. Clicking on an item in the list will show that item selected in the preview window to the right.

3 On the Order and Timing tab, the Animation Order box holds the order in which the objects you have ticked will be animated. Click on an object and then on the Move buttons to change the order it will be displayed in. If a background object appears after foreground objects it will be placed behind them, and vice versa.

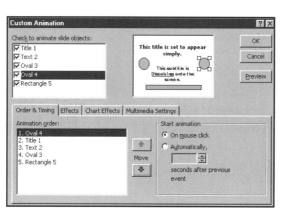

4 You can click Preview at any time to see the slide animation displayed in its entirety in the preview window.

ANIMATION EFFECTS

There are 17 different animations that you can select from, most of which allow you to choose a secondary setting, such as the direction from which the effect is to be applied. A limited selection of these animations (complete with pre-set options) is available from the Preset Animation submenu of the SLIDE SHOW menu.

1 With an object selected in the Custom Animation dialog and ticked for animation, switch to the Effects tab. The area marked as Entry animation and sound will be active.

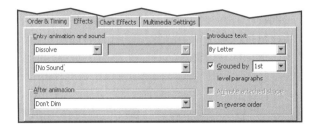

2 Click on the Effect Style box, top left in the Entry Animation and Sound area, for a drop-down menu of the 17 different effect types. Scroll through it and click on one to apply it.

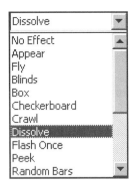

3 Sub-options will be listed in the drop-down selection box directly to the right of the Effect Style box. Click on this to open another pick list, generally of possible directions to apply the effect from.

4 You can also add a sound to the animation from the pick list below the Effect Style box. Once again, click on it and select one. No Sound and Stop Previous Sound, as their names suggest, attach no sound to the animation. The bottom option, Other Sound... allows you to choose a sound file from your hard drive.

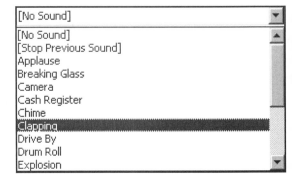

STAGED APPEARANCES

From the <u>Effects</u> tab, you can also choose to have the items you animate dim after their appearance. In the <u>After Animation</u> tab, click on the drop-down list to get a selection of colours that you can apply as semi-transparent colouring to each item on the slide once it has been animated. If a colour is chosen, the item will become that colour once the next animation starts on that slide. If you pick <u>Hide After Animation</u>, the object will vanish as soon as its animation has completed. If you pick <u>Hide on Next Mouse Click</u>, the object will vanish once the next animation starts, as with the colour. The default option is <u>Don't Dim</u>, which means that nothing more happens to the object once the animation is complete.

The <u>Introduce Text</u> area allows you to select different options for displaying text. The main dropdown pick list, set by default to <u>All at once</u>, allows you to choose whether the text is animated as one block, as individual words or as individual letters. The <u>Grouped by...</u> checkbox is rather misleadingly named. If you select this, individual bullet points will be treated as separate animations. Pick a bullet rank from the dropdown list beside it; all bullets of that rank and above will be treated separately. Bullets below that rank will be displayed with the higher-ranking bullets above them.

In conjunction with the <u>After Animation</u> pick-list, the <u>Grouped by Nth Level Paragraphs</u> tick box allows you to perform the classic PowerPoint trick of introducing bullets one at a time on a slide, and having them dim out when the next bullet appears – extremely handy for directing audience attention.

You can choose from a number of colours and effects to apply to an object post-animation.

These bullets can enter one by one

Note how bullets in place are greyed out!

* Bullet 1

* Bullet 2

* Bullet 3

  • Bullet 4

ANIMATION TIMING

Each different object's animation can be timed separately within the slide.

1 From the Order & Timing tab, you have access to the Start animation area. This is where each individual animation's timing options are set.

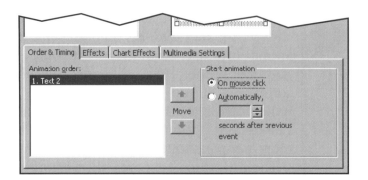

2 The default option for the Start animation setting is On mouse click. In this instance, the slide's animation sequence will pause at the end of the animation until the mouse is clicked. You can also time the animation to occur a certain period of time after the previous event finishes by clicking the Automatically... radio button and entering a time in minutes and seconds into the box below it.

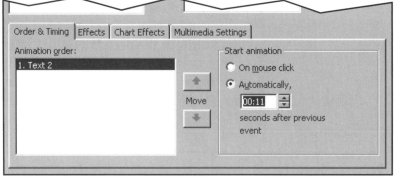

TIMING NOTE

You should bear in mind that if the slides in your Slide Show are set to advance after a certain period of time, slide animations will no longer wait for a mouse click, even though the slide's time will not be up until the slide animations are complete. If no timing is set for the animations, they will be triggered immediately, one after another. You can set a timed delay, however, and clicking with the mouse will over-ride the timed delay, so you can achieve the same effect by setting a really long Automatically... time in the Start animation area, and then clicking when you are ready.

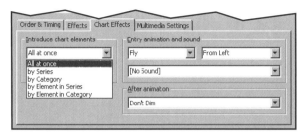

You can animate various chart elements with the Chart Effects tab.

CHART AND MULTIMEDIA OPTIONS

Charts and multimedia clips both have their own special-case animation options. If the slide holds a chart, the Chart Effects tab of the Custom Animation dialog is going to be active; similarly, if the slide holds a sound or movie file, the Multimedia Settings tab is going to be active.

From the Chart Effects tab, the Introduce Chart Elements drop-down pick list allows you to select how the chart's data series are going to be introduced – as the whole chart together, by whole series or categories or as individual elements in series or category order. If you select Animate Grid and Legend then the chart's background will appear in the style of the animation; if you do not select it, it will just appear in place as soon as the chart animation begins. The Entry Animation and Sound area and After Animation area function in the same way as normal elements, although the range of available effects is slightly smaller for chart objects.

The Multimedia Settings tab allows you to decide how the external clip is going to be handled. When a multimedia clip is inserted onto a slide, you have the option of choosing whether it will play as soon as the slide is accessed, or whether it will become active when clicked on. The Play using animation order tick-box on the tab overrides this, allowing you to assign a normal animation order to the clip's activation. You can then use the While Playing radio buttons to choose whether the Slide Show animation pauses for the clip or continues with it while the slide plays, and the Stop Playing buttons allow you to set a maximum duration in slides for the clip to play for. The More Options button allows you to decide whether the clip will loop continually or not, or whether a movie is returned to the first frame when it ends.

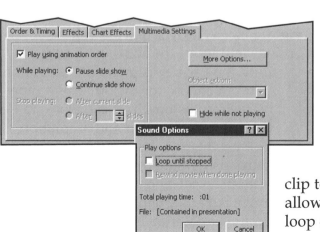

S WITCHING SLIDES

Just as each individual slide can be animated to add interest, the Slide Show itself can be extensively customised according to your needs. You can assign hyperlinks to objects, leap around the presentation – even call up entirely different slide shows.

SETTING UP THE SHOW

The basic running options for the Slide Show are set from the Set Up Show dialog box, accessed by clicking Set Up Show from the SLIDE SHOW menu. To the left of the dialog, the Show type area allows you to choose the basic defining settings of the show. The default option is a show that is Presented by a speaker, where right-clicking the mouse provides options and the show can be manipulated. The Browsed by an individual option sets the show up a bit like a web browser display, with a progress Scrollbar that can be disabled by unticking it. Finally, Browsed at a kiosk disables all external access options and loops the show continuously until the Esc key is pressed – an option you can choose for the other two types by ticking the box. You can also choose to suppress narration and animation. You can restrict the show to a range of slides using the From or Custom radio buttons in the Slides are and, if you move Advance Slides from Using timings to Manually, then regardless of what timing options you set, slides and

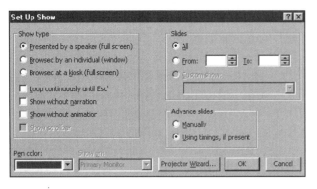

animations will progress only by a mouse click. The Projector Wizard helps you set up a show on a data projector, which you must already have connected to the computer.

CONTROLLING SLIDES

You have a number of key options open to you for controlling your Slide Show manually when it is running in full-screen mode. Pressing Enter, Page Down, the Right arrow, the Down arrow, Space or N will start the next animation or move to the next slide. To re-show the previous animation or go to the previous slide, you can press Page Up, Left arrow, Up arrow, Backspace or P. To jump directly to a slide, type in its number in the presentation and press Enter. Pressing B or '.' will pause the slideshow, displaying a black screen, and pressing W or ',' will pause it with a white screen. Pressing S or '+' will simply pause the show in mid-flow. To end the show completely, you can press Esc, Ctrl-Break or '-'. If you want to return to the start, press down both mouse buttons simultaneously, and hold them down for two seconds. If you need to delete the annotations you have made with the pen tool, you can press E to erase them. If you have hidden a slide – that is, set it not to appear in the show – but decide that you need it, you can press H to jump to the next Hidden slide in the presentation. Pressing Ctrl-P will display the pointer as a pen, while pressing Ctrl-A will display it as an arrow, Ctrl-H will hide it right away and Ctrl-U will hide it after waiting 15 seconds. Pressing Tab will select the next hyperlink on a slide (starting with the first), while Shift-Tab will select the last and then previous hyperlinks. If you need more control, right-clicking the mouse, or pressing Shift-F10 will bring up the Slide Show shortcut menu. Once a Hyperlink is selected, you can press Enter to activate it as if you had clicked on it, or Shift-Enter to show what happens when the mouse pointer passes over it.

HANDY TIP

If you forget all of that, never fear — you can press F1 during the Slide Show to get a full list of key commands at your disposal.

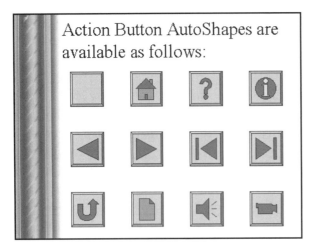

INTRODUCTION TO ACTION BUTTONS

Action buttons are special Drawing Objects that have a built-in action attached to them that is activated when they are clicked, or when the mouse pointer passes over them. These actions vary, but can include playing a sound, jumping to another point in the presentation or even hyperlinking to an entirely different document or program all together. There are several Action Button AutoShapes which work in the same way but vary in appearance in order to make the function you intend to assign to them more intuitive for someone else using the presentation.

In addition to the action buttons, you can also assign actions to an object by right-clicking on it and selecting Action Settings from the pop-up menu that appears. This gives you a little more flexibility that just having to use the pre-defined Action Button AutoShapes.

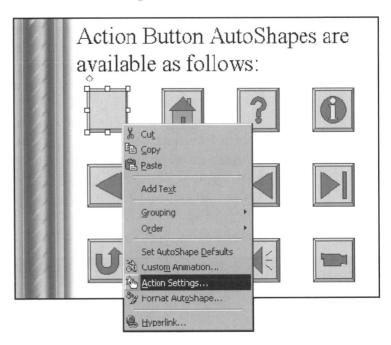

The Action Settings option is also available by right-clicking on an object.

ACTIONS

When you assign an action to an object – or when you place an Action Button on a slide, as PowerPoint automatically assigns an action to every new Action Button – the <u>Action Settings</u> dialog box appears. It has two tabs, <u>Mouse Click</u> and <u>Mouse Over</u>. The settings chosen for the <u>Mouse Click</u> tab activate when the button or object is clicked on with the mouse during a <u>Slide Show</u> and, following suit, the <u>Mouse Over</u> tab settings are activated when the mouse pointer moves on to or over the button or object. Aside from that, the two tabs are almost identical.

   If you want to, you can attach a sound to either or both of the <u>Click</u> and <u>Over</u> options, independently of any action you may set. You can also choose to have the object or button highlighted in either instance, too, although this latter option is set on for <u>Action Buttons</u>. The most significant area of the

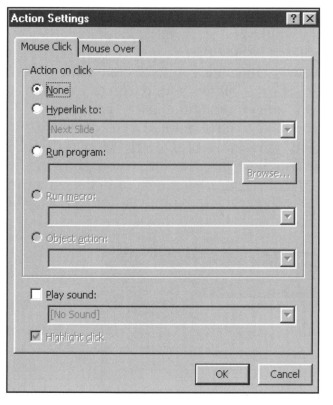

Action Settings dialog, however, is the <u>Action on click</u> area, called <u>Action on mouse over</u> in the <u>Mouse Over</u> tab. From this section, you can select the action to perform. <u>None</u> is the default, and does exactly what it says – nothing. <u>Hyperlink to</u>: allows you to use the action to jump to another slide or document. <u>Run program</u> calls an external program – with a command line you specify – to run in the background while your presentation continues. You use a dialog box similar to the standard <u>Open File</u> dialog to locate the program you want to run. If you have any macros in your presentation (we'll look at macros later) you can attach one of those to the action. Finally, you can also use the action to perform an OLE operation.

HYPERLINK ACTIONS

When you select <u>Hyperlink to</u>: for an action, you also need to select the destination for that hyperlink. There are a number of options that you have available in order to use the hyperlink effectively.

To add a hyperlink action, click on the <u>Hyperlink to</u> radio button. You can then click on the drop-down pick list box to

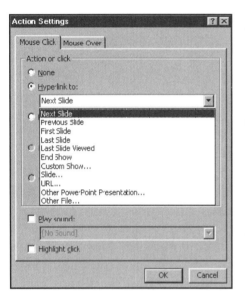

select a hyperlink destination. <u>Next Slide</u> and <u>Previous Slide</u>, the top two options, refer to the slides immediately after and before the current one in the Slide Show respectively. If the current slide is 6, the previous slide is number 5, even if there was a hyperlink to the current slide. <u>First Slide</u> and <u>Last Slide</u> refer to the start and end slides of the show, and these actions will take you right back to the beginning or all the way to the finish. <u>Last Slide Viewed</u> takes you back a step, to the last slide you saw before the current one – useful if your Slide Show has a lot of hyperlinks. <u>End Show</u> does just that, stops the show completely, returning you to Normal view. <u>Custom Show…</u> allows you to leap to a custom sub-set of the presentation. Before you can use this, you have to have defined a custom show, by selecting <u>Custom Shows</u> from the <u>SLIDE SHOW</u> menu and selecting the slides and their order for the custom show. <u>Slide…</u> opens the <u>Slide Selector</u> dialog box; from this, you can pick a specific slide to hyperlink to by title or number, and this will ensure the action always links to that slide.

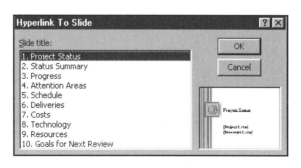

You can hyperlink to a specific slide in your presentation with the <u>Hyperlink To Slide</u> dialog box.

EXTERNAL HYPERLINKS

There are three external hyperlink functions provided by the Action Settings dialog box. These, as the name suggests, do not link to a place within the current presentation at all. Other PowerPoint Presentation... shows you an Open File dialog box so you can attach a link to an entirely different presentation. If you want to use more than one design template or more than one set of Master Slides within a Slide Show, you will have to use this function and hyperlink to a different presentation, as any one file can only have one design template.

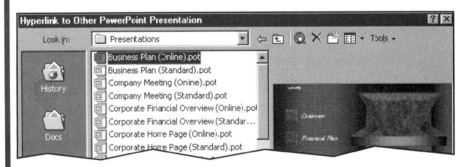

Selecting URL... opens the Hyperlink to URL dialog box. Perhaps surprisingly, this is just a simple text entry box. There are no cross-links to Internet Explorer or Microsoft Outlook, and you cannot select one of your Web Favourites or Bookmarks automatically. You have to type the Hyperlink URL into the box, the old-fashioned way! If the computer is not connected to the Internet when this action is activated (i.e. the button is clicked), it will attempt to open a connection.

Finally, you can Hyperlink to an external file with the Other File... option. An Open File dialog lets you select the file you want to link to. When the action is activated from a Slide Show, the document will be called up in its own program and the Slide Show temporarily put on hold. As soon as the active focus of Windows returns to PowerPoint – if the external program is closed maybe or minimized – the presentation will continue.

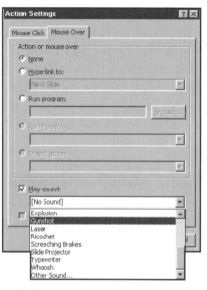

CONSIDERATIONS

It can be somewhat risky assigning actions to objects, particularly Hyperlinks and program executions. One major consideration is using the <u>Mouse Over</u> functions. If you set a <u>Mouse Over</u> to trigger a Hyperlink, you may well find yourself leaping to slides, files or even other systems that you did not particularly want to visit if your mouse cursor strays over the trigger object by mistake. It is better to stick to using the <u>Mouse Over</u> functions to pop up an alert or some descriptive text.

In addition, if you do link to an external file, document or presentation, you need to be absolutely certain that the document or program is going to stay where you put it. If it moves or is renamed, or if your presentation is accessed on a different computer from the one you created it on, you might lose functionality to external program links. Even worse, a different document or file might have the same name as the one you used, and calling that program by mistake could, theoretically, cause all sorts of crashes. If you don't need to create external links, then it's best not to. Finally, a thought – you can take a leaf from the web site designers' book and include a set of action buttons

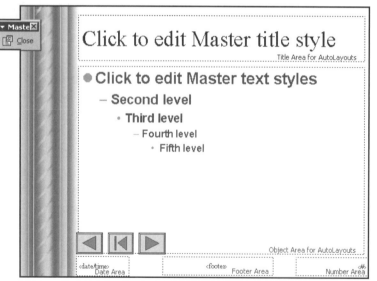

for simple hyperlink functions, such as back, home, forward and end, and place them on the Slide Masters. That way the buttons, and the actions, will be available from every slide, reliably visible and consistent. If other people are going to be browsing your Slide Show, this can be very useful indeed.

SLIDE TRANSITIONS

Transitions, like animations, are a way of livening up your Slide Show. In an abstract sense, the transition is the time between one slide being advanced and the next slide actually appearing on the screen. If you do not select any particular transitions, then this process will be more or less instantaneous. However, there are 40 different transition options, based around 12 main transition types. Like animations, each of them is a short animated sequence to delineate the end of one slide and the beginning of the next; and, also like animations, transitions are only visible during a Slide Show. Transitions can be accessed by selecting <u>Slide Transition</u> from the <u>SLIDE SHOW</u> menu.

The <u>Effect</u> area of the <u>Slide Transition</u> dialog allows you to pick one of the different transition types. Click on the dropdown pick list and select a transition that takes your fancy. <u>No Transition</u>, the default, leaves slides switching simply between one another, while <u>Random Transition</u>, the last option, will pick a transition effect at random each time that transition is activated. You can set the relative speed of the transition with the <u>Slow</u>, <u>Medium</u> and <u>Fast</u> radio buttons below the pick list box. The picture above the pick list box serves as a preview, demonstrating the transition every time it is selected or modified.

SLIDE ADVANCEMENT

The Slide Transition dialog box includes the settings area for applying a blanket timing to each slide.

1 To apply a slide transition time, go to the Advance area of the Slide Transition dialog box and tick the Automatically after check box. This will then activate the timing entry box. You can type in a time in minutes and seconds here, or use the up and down arrows to set a time.

2 When you have a time that suits you, click Apply to All to set this time as the new default for the Slide Show. Unless you have deactivated the option in the Slide Set Up dialog box (activated from the SLIDE SHOW menu), the new timing will be used in the Slide Show in addition to the mouse click function. Take care, though, as any transition effects you have selected will also be applied at the same time.

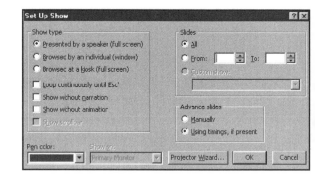

3 You can check your new slide timings – and verify whether or not you have set any transitions – from the Slide Sorter view. Activating the sorter will show you automatic advancement times and transitions for each slide, if they are present, as a value and a small slide icon respectively, just below the bottom left hand corner of each slide in the view.

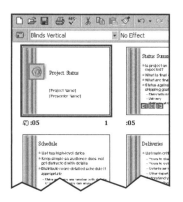

TRANSITIONARY EFFECTS

There are a dozen broad classes of different effects available as slide transition options. Blinds take the form of five or six lines on the screen which advance simultaneously, painting the new slide behind them. Box transitions start from the centre or the edges of the slide and move smoothly across the old slide, expanding or contracting respectively. Checkerboards divide the slide into a grid and fill each alternate box in simultaneously in a chessboard pattern before going back and filling the squares left out the last time in the same way. Cover moves the new slide over the old one, while Uncover drags the old one off the new one. Cut just snaps straight to the next slide. Dissolve paints the new slide on pixel by pixel in random order. Random bars do the same, only in lines across the screen rather than single points. Fade through black wipes the slide out based on a grid, then paints the new one back on in the same way. Splits paint the new slide in two simultaneous halves. Strips wipe across the slide from one corner to the other. Wipe is a straight line that goes across the screen replacing the old with the new. Random, finally, selects one of the 40 specific options at random each time it is called upon. Select the transition you want, and Apply it.

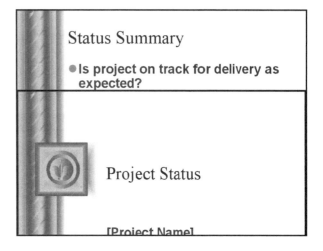

Transitions cut from one slide to the next using attractive animations such as Dissolve (above) and Uncover (right).

SOUND

You can elect to have each slide transition marked by a PowerPoint sound being played. Within the <u>Sound</u> area, click on the drop-down pick list to get a list of the default sounds that PowerPoint uses. [No Sound] will not play a sound at the transition, while [Stop Previous Sound] will also terminate any other PowerPoint sound that is playing.

Pick one you like, or click on the <u>Other Sound…</u> option to get a file dialog that will allow you to pick a specific sound file from your computer. Remember to highlight it and click <u>OK</u> to select it.

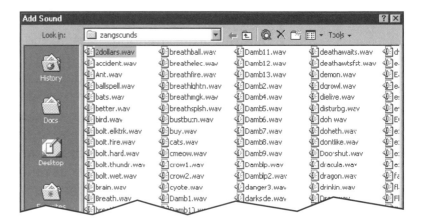

Once you have chosen a sound, you can also tick the <u>Loop until next sound</u> button, below the pick list. If you do so, the sound will be continually repeated until the next sound is encountered.

APPLYING TRANSITIONS AND ADVANCES TO ONE SLIDE

If you want to use the <u>Slide Transition</u> dialog box to change just one slide, you have to make sure that slide is the active one first – that is, that the slide you want to modify is the one on the slide display screen in <u>Normal</u> view, or the one with the blue outline around it in <u>Slide Sorter</u> view. At that point, you can select <u>Slide Transitions</u>, pick your new option, and click on the <u>Apply</u> button – not the <u>Apply to All</u> button, which will set the entire presentation to those options. There is no way of selecting the active slide from within the <u>Slide Transition</u> dialog box.

B LISTERING SHOWS

When the time comes to give a presentation, all your hard work preparing slides and transitions is going to be severely undermined if you have not mastered your speech. This book is about teaching you how to use PowerPoint to its full advantage rather than about public speaking, but fortunately the program includes several useful tools to help you get to grips with a speech and make the most of the occasion. In this chapter we'll look at rehearsing slide timing, adding narration and using the Meeting Minder to keep notes.

REHEARSING A SLIDE SHOW

Even the most informal meeting or presentation is going to have some sort of time limit. Given that the average professional adult has an average focused attendance span of around 20 minutes and a cut-off point around three-quarters of an hour, you'll lose half your audience by the time you've been presenting for 30 minutes. PowerPoint's rehearsal functions allow you to check the timing of your speech, and to set the timed advances to fit your needs, slide by slide.

REHEARSE TIMINGS

The principle behind a rehearsal is simple. PowerPoint runs the show as normal, advancing animations or slides only when you click the mouse button. Each time you move forward a slide, it makes a note of how long you left it before advancing. When you have finished, it has a record of exactly how long you took to click through the presentation, and how long you spent on each slide. The idea is that you run through your speech while the rehearsal is going on, so you can time exactly how long you need for each slide. You can then choose to apply these timings to the slides when the show is over. This can be extremely useful if you will be giving the speech in a situation where you will not actually have control over the computer displaying the show.

Different slides can have different timings.

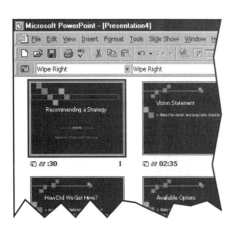

RUNNING A REHEARSAL

Before you start a rehearsal, it is worth making sure that you have a full set of speaker's notes handy, or at least a print-out of the slides, so that you know what is coming. If you know you have a time limit for the presentation, bear it in mind and try to work out how to pace yourself so that you use your time effectively.

1 To start a rehearsal, click on Rehearse Timings from the initially hidden selections on the SLIDE SHOW menu.

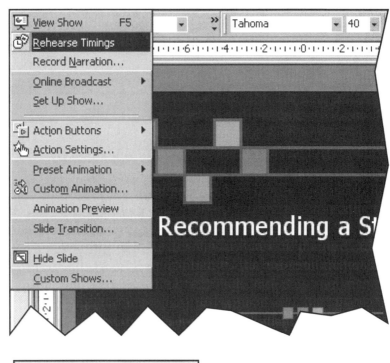

2 The slide show will start as normal, except that the Rehearsal toolbar will be visible in the corner of the screen. This provides you with the Next, Pause, Slide Time, Repeat and Show Time functions respectively.

3 To move on to the next animation item or the next slide, click the left mouse button or click on the Next icon on the tool bar. The time you have taken on each slide, including animation time, is shown in the Slide Time indicator. If you need to start the slide again, click the Repeat button to zero that slide's time and the time it has contributed to the total show time.

PAUSING REHEARSAL

The slide rehearsal process can be temporarily suspended by clicking on the <u>Pause</u> button on the <u>Rehearsal</u> toolbar. When you click this button, the progress of the slide's animations is halted, and the system stops the counter. You should note, though, that many of the actual animated sequences cannot be paused or interrupted by even low-level Windows functions, so if you click <u>Pause</u> in the middle of a Dissolve or Spiral (for example), that particular animation will continue until complete before pausing. Once the slide has been paused, the <u>Pause</u> button is clicked on.

You can resume the rehearsal by clicking on the <u>Pause</u> button a second time. Clicking one of the other buttons on the toolbar will resume the count as well, but it will also perform whatever effect is normally assigned to the button you click – so if you click <u>Repeat</u> to restart the slide, its count will be reset to zero. There are other slide functions that you can perform that will pause the rehearsal, though. Right-clicking the mouse to get the popup shortcut <u>Slide Show</u> menu will pause the count until the menu has been closed. Selecting the pen tool will also pause the count – the time that you spend annotating the slide will not be acknowledged. In fact in general, using the pen counts as having the entire Slide Show paused. You can resume by clicking on the <u>Pause</u> button, or by resetting the cursor to <u>Default</u>, <u>Hidden</u> or <u>Arrow</u>.

ANIMATIONS AND THE PEN

Pen annotations are not just erased when the slide changes. They are also erased when an object animation starts, so if you want your annotations to last for the slide's duration, make sure you do not draw them until after the whole slide has been annotated.

APPLYING REHEARSAL TIMES

When the Slide Show ends, or when you close the Rehearsal toolbar, you will be offered the option of applying the time you have taken, slide by slide, to the Slide Show defaults, setting the time for each slide to that of your rehearsal. A dialog box will tell you the total time taken and ask you if you want to apply the new times from your Rehearsal. Click Yes to apply them, or No to leave them as they are.

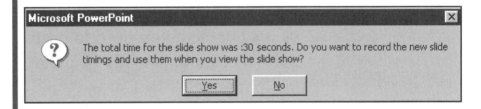

One thing that you should be aware of is that slides which are timed do not make allowance for timing object animations. If you want to time the appearance of each of the objects on a timed slide, you cannot do it using the automatic timing functions. However, you can fake it convincingly. If you want to time object animations, first make sure that each item you want to animate is a separate object; then copy the slide once for each object and apply the new animation on each slide. In other words, if you wanted to time the appearance of individual animated bullets to fit in with the timing of your speech then, rather than one three-item bullet list set for grouped appearance, you would need to create three neatly-aligned one-bullet text boxes. You then duplicate the slide once for each object to animate after the first, so there is one slide for each object you are animating. Next you delete all but the first item on the first slide, all but the first two items on the second slide and so on. Set the duplicate slides to have no transition between them; then animate the new object on each duplicate slide – bullet one on slide one, bullet two on slide two and so on. You can even colour the old items differently to simulate dimming-out. When you run the show, the set of slides will appear to be one internally-animated one.

ADDING NARRATION

PowerPoint includes an effective tool for allowing you to add narration to your Slide Show, which can be invaluable if you need to prepare a presentation that you cannot actually be present for. Over the next few pages, we'll look at the topic of narration in depth, considering when and why to add it, what you need to do so, how to do it, and even how to undo it if you make a mistake.

HOW DOES NARRATION WORK?

As the name suggests, adding narration to a slide involves recording dialogue that is then played when the Slide Show is activated. In other words, your speech is recorded along with

This slide includes narration

This is shown by the Sound Object
(the speaker icon) in the bottom right
hand corner of the slide.

the slides, on a slide-by-slide basis. As with rehearsals, the time that you use for each slide is fixed as the defaults for the show. It works by creating a new sound file for each slide. The contents of that sound are recorded via a microphone plugged into your computer's sound card. When the slide is advanced, the file you are recording is closed, the time that slide took is saved and a new sound file, which is actually attached to the new slide, is started.

WHEN TO USE NARRATION

In general, it is going to be better to present material live and in person. Audiences do not respond particularly well to a pre-recorded speech – at least, not unless it includes TV-quality images, and even then a visible narrator is the norm, so as to hold interest. However, if that isn't an option, if you can't be there in person to make the speech that goes with the presentation, then recording a narration is far better than just running a Slide Show without it. A display monitor at a convention booth, for example, may well have to be unattended, and a narration for a PowerPoint presentation could then make all the difference.

MULTIPLE NARRATION

PowerPoint will not, unfortunately, allow you to record more than one narration sound file per slide. You can't persuade the system to allow you to attach narration sounds to individual animations, mouse clicks or timings. If you need to leave a long pause between narrative comments on a slide, you're going to have to record silence, at 10K of disk space per second... But, as with timed animations, you can also fake it. If you duplicate a slide several times and choose not to display a transition between its instances, then advancing the slide will be invisible, and you can attach a different narration to each version of the slide, providing you (in effect) with multiple narrative comments. If you then make the slide display time longer than the narration time, you will get silences you can use without having to devote valuable disk space to them.

THE RECORD NARRATION DIALOG

Assuming that your preparations are complete – your
equipment is set up properly, and your Slide Show is complete
– then adding narration is simple.

1 Select <u>Record Narration...</u> from the <u>SLIDE SHOW</u> menu. It is one of the options that is hidden by default, so you may need to click the down arrows on the menu. The <u>Record Narration</u> dialog box will appear. The <u>Current recording quality</u> area will show you the amount of space your narration sound files will take up, also indicating the free disk space you have, and the maximum amount of time that space could give you. The default options are for radio-quality narration, generally fine for speech, which takes 10K per second. CD-quality narration would take up 172K per second, so is rarely an option.

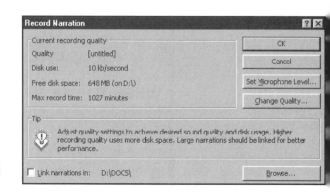

2 You can change the sound quality by clicking <u>Change Quality...</u>. This will show you a dialog called <u>Sound Selection</u>. Click on the <u>Attributes</u> pick-list to get a selection of different quality options. The lower down the list the options you select, the higher the quality but the more disk space used. Do not alter any of the other settings.

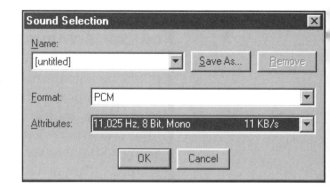

3 You can check the microphone is ready and working by clicking <u>Microphone Level...</u> This will show you a <u>Microphone Check</u> box with a volume slider. Speak into it, and you'll hear what you say over the computer speakers at the volume chosen. If nothing happens, check your microphone is plugged into your sound card's Mic input, or ask your IT support for help. When you are ready to record narration, click <u>OK</u>.

APPLYING NARRATION

Once you start recording narration, your Slide Show will start as normal. Slide timings will be temporarily disabled, so you will have to use the left mouse button to advance the animations and slides as if you were rehearsing the show. Once the Slide Show is complete, you'll see a query alert against a black screen telling you that the narrations have been saved for each slide, and asking if you want to apply slide timings too. If you select <u>Yes</u>, the time you took for each slide will be applied to that slide for the Slide Show timings, just as if it was a rehearsal. If not, the timing will be left in its current state.

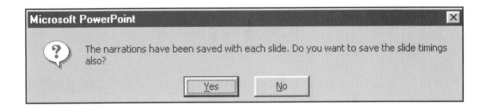

Narration files are set to play automatically and to continue playing until they are complete or the next slide is opened. These options are set in the <u>Custom Animation</u> dialog, and can be modified from there too. They are represented in each slide by a small Sound File object icon in the bottom right-hand corner of the file.

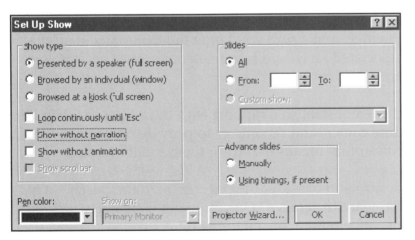

DISABLING NARRATION

You can deactivate all slide narrations from the <u>Set Up Show</u> dialog box, accessed from the <u>SLIDE SHOW</u> menu. The <u>Show type</u> area includes a checkbox option to <u>Show without narration</u>. Tick this and click <u>OK</u> to disable the show's narration.

GOOD PRESENTATIONS

Although we don't have the space in this book to go into details of how to master the delicate art of giving a presentation, there are a number of useful tips that will stand you in good stead. Try to follow them wherever possible.

- First and foremost, remember the Four Ps of making any speech:

    Plan: make sure you know what you want to say, and that you are aware of the opinions and biases of your audience.

    Prepare: try to make sure that your presentation timing is balanced; that you're not labouring some points and skimping others.

    Practice: make sure you know the material and all the associated facts, and rehearse your speech so that you are confident with it.

    Present: establish a rapport with the audience when the time comes, and remember to provide occasional conceptual breaks to refresh their attention span.

- Make sure you consider the purpose of your speech – what do you want to achieve? Do you want to change people's minds, inform them or sell to them?

- Don't over-estimate your audience, but don't patronise them either. Make sure they can understand what you're saying. Try to use jargon that they themselves use.

- Make sure that you yourself are fully aware of the value of what you are saying, and why it is important to you. It will give you conviction.

- Every so often, fall back on some key points to summarize what you've been saying. This is a good time to provide a bullet list slide.

- Remember to prepare evidence to back up any data claims.

- Grab attention when you start by shocking your audience, passing on an interesting tale, or making them think about a question.

- Similarly, make sure you close on a high note by summarizing surprising conclusions, shadowing back to your opening or challenging your audience – and always make sure you tell them what you want them to take away from the speech, and/or what they have to do now.

- Ask a friend to help you by listening to your speech and giving you feedback.

- Try to make eye contact with your audience. Speak naturally, conversationally, but without "umms" and "ahhs". Slow down for important issues, and pause before and after vital points to emphasize them.

- Don't take questions during the speech unless you absolutely have to; it will throw off your timing. If you plan to take questions afterwards, prepare and practice answers to the questions you expect and try to recruit a colleague to sit in the audience and ask the first question for you, to get the ball rolling.

THE MEETING MINDER

During a PowerPoint presentation, particularly if you are using it as the focus of a meeting, you will often find that you need to keep a record of comments, ideas, action points and other items that arise in conversation. You can, of course, make notes in the old-fashioned way with pencil and paper. However, you can also use the built-in Meeting Minder to keep track of action points for you.

Minutes exported from the Meeting Minder.

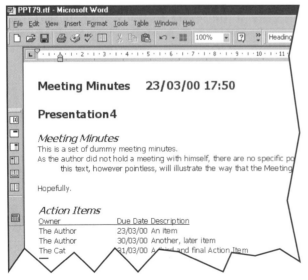

USING THE MEETING MINDER

The Meeting Minder allows you to track comments and action points simply and effectively, and to export them either to a scheduling program, or to save them out as a text file. You can run the Meeting Minder equally as effectively from the normal operation of PowerPoint as from a Slide Show, too. To call up the Meeting Minder from within PowerPoint, select Meeting Minder from the TOOLS menu. To access it from a Slide Show, right-click the mouse button and select Meeting Minder from the popup shortcut menu that appears. When the Meeting Minder is open, as with the shortcut menu itself, the Slide Show timing is paused, so that you can enter your comments as necessary.

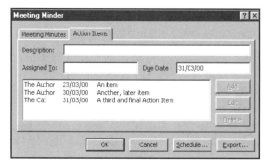

ACTION ITEMS

When you start the Meeting Minder, a dialog box will appear on the screen. This has two different areas; the <u>Meeting Minutes</u> tab and the <u>Action Items</u> tab. The more versatile of these is the Action Items tab, so we'll look at that first.

Assigning an action item is easy.

1 First of all, click in the <u>Description</u> box and type the action item that you want to assign.

2 Next, identify the person to take the action in the <u>Assigned To</u> box, and if the completion date is after today, modify the date in the <u>Due Date</u> box.

3 Finally, click on <u>Add</u> to insert the action into the list.

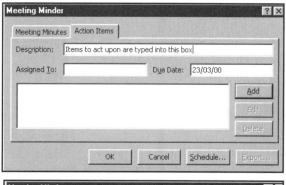

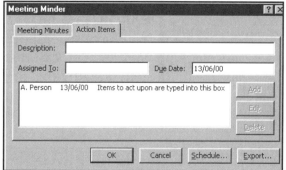

You can click on an item in the list and select <u>Edit</u> to move it out of the list and back into the boxes, so that you can modify it and press <u>Add</u> again, or you can click on the item and press <u>Delete</u> to get rid of it. Action items will automatically be added to a new, appropriately-titled slide at the end of the presentation, using default formatting and any design templates or master styles that are available. This is actually where they are stored when the Meeting Minder is inactive, so making changes will change the items in the Minder too.

MEETING MINUTES

The <u>Meeting Minutes</u> tab operates on a much simpler basis. You simply click inside the box, and type. You cannot apply any formatting or tabs, but you can enter the full range of letters, punctuation, returns and so on. The <u>Meeting Minutes</u> tab can hold up to 4,096 characters of information, which should be sufficient for most meetings. Minutes are not stored on a slide, but kept in memory by the computer.

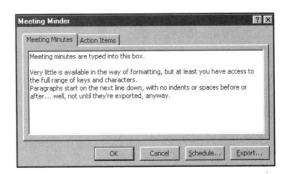

EXPORTING NOTES

You have several options to export data from the Meeting Minder. You can restrict yourself to using the automatic slide generated by the <u>Actions Points</u> tab, and just printing that out. You can also click on the <u>Schedule</u> button to bring up Microsoft Outlook, if you have it installed, so that you can create a schedule for an action point or meeting item. Finally, you can click on <u>Export</u> to call up the <u>Meeting Minder Export</u> dialog, which will allow you to transmit all the Meeting Minutes and Action Items to a pre-formatted Microsoft Word document for printing, saving or distributing as appropriate, as in the picture on page 146. Tick the options you require and click <u>Export Now</u> to do so.

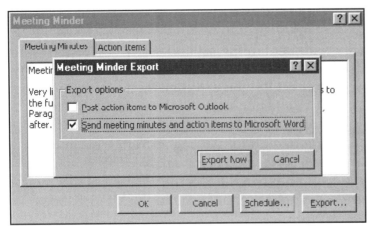

BEING HEARD

9

PowerPoint is a great tool for communication. It provides you with many different ways of getting your messages across clearly and effectively, of making what you want to say stand out, so that the maximum number of people can hear you clearly. Communicating, of course, involves other people. In this chapter, we'll look at some of the less common ways that PowerPoint can be used to reach out to others – both on and offline.

POWERPOINT AND DTP

Desktop Publishing, or DTP, is one of the most significant aspects of the computer revolution. For the first time, everyone can acquire the means to put their ideas and comments across clearly and professionally without having to resort to expensive physical production. The printing press changed the world by making books accessible, and DTP is changing it again.

The Spiral

Escape The Maze

Representation and Financial Services to take the Hassle out of Professional Creative Careers

WHAT IS DESKTOP PUBLISHING?

DTP is the combined result of several different strands provided by modern computers. It can be thought of as a blend of word processing, automated text layout, easy access to graphical illustration, design and page layout functions and sophisticated personal printers. Before modern techniques were available, each page of a brochure, book or other document had to be assembled in a press, by professional typesetters and printers, as a metal plate made out of small letter blocks and larger illustration etchings. This was then smeared with ink and pressed against paper. By making **every** stage of that process electronically automated for you, DTP gives you access to your very own small printing and design press – and you can produce any sort of document you like with it. The only real limit lies in the sophistication of your printer.

COMMON DESKTOP PUBLISHING TASKS

In practice, of course, the printing equipment needed to reproduce realistic colour photographs and illustrations is extraordinarily expensive, and so big that it doesn't really fit anywhere near your desktop. However, that won't often prove particularly restricting, and you can always take your files to a print shop for professional output. DTP is truly versatile, and finds many solutions around the home and office. Notices, small posters and other display items are probably the classic DTP solution. Just a few years ago, even simple flyers had to be printed for you by professional printing companies. Nowadays you can design a poster and run off 50 copies in a matter of minutes.

Another common use for DTP is in producing forms – application forms, survey questionnaires, report slips and so on. Pitch documents, business reports and plans, certificates – all can be swiftly and easily created on screen and printed. Even sophisticated brochures are easily accomplished using DTP software, although the printing might still be done by dedicated professionals. Any time you produce a paper document for public use, that's DTP in action.

POWERPOINT AND DESKTOP PUBLISHING

Although PowerPoint was originally designed as a program to support meetings, as all the terminology of Slides, Presentations, Slide Shows and the rest reminds us, it also makes a great DTP application. There are just a few things that you need to bear in mind when using it as such.

1 The default page you work on in PowerPoint is sized specially for an on-screen slide. The ratio between that and the paper you are printing on may not be exact – particularly in the UK, where we use A4 size paper, 210x297mm, rather than the US standard Letter size, 216x279mm. Because A4 is longer, it is difficult to rescale exactly.

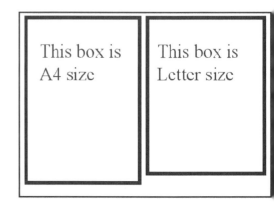

This box is A4 size

This box is Letter size

2 Before using PowerPoint for DTP work, make sure that the slide size matches the paper size. You can adjust the slide size from the Page Setup dialog, accessed via the FILE menu. Select your paper size from the Slides sized for dropdown menu. The Width and Height boxes take into account PowerPoint's pre-set margins, the gap between the edge of the paper and the start of the text. You may find it more realistic to type the paper's actual dimensions into these boxes – 21cm Width and 29.7cm Height for A4 paper.

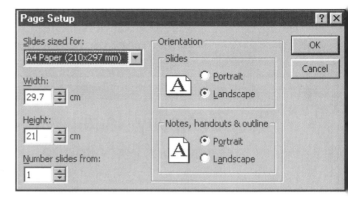

3 You need to make sure that your slide's orientation – the way up it is – matches the way you want it to appear on the paper. If you want the paper vertical, (the normal way), set the Slides Orientation to the Portrait radio button. If you prefer it horizontal, like a banner, leave it at Landscape.

DTP STRENGTHS AND LIMITATIONS OF POWERPOINT

PowerPoint is extremely simple and user-friendly. It goes out of its way to make everything as quick and easy as it can, and glosses over a lot of the trivial details of design for you in order to get you up and running. The grid that objects automatically snap to when you move them makes it really easy to line different slide elements up, so that everything looks neat and efficient. The different pick-list palettes for line styles, colours, special fill templates and colour schemes take all the hassle out of design for you. PowerPoint also provides a lot of support for quick access to a wide range of graphic illustrations through Clip Art, charts, AutoShapes, Word Art and more, and offers you a great selection of well-balanced design templates to make everything look really pretty. This is a great strength, but it is also a weakness. Where the program handles the specifics for you to make things accessible, you lose flexibility and true power. You can resize your text really quickly and easily – but you can't give it a double-underline, or automatically set it so that lower-case letters display as little capital letters, as you can in Word. You can create an 8, 16, 24 or even 32-pointed star at the click of one button, but creating a geometrically-perfect 9-pointed star is almost impossible. The grid lets you line objects up really quickly, but it does mean that you can't misalign something ever so slightly for artistic effect. The design templates give you immediate access to great-looking graphic styles, but there aren't *that* many of them, and they quickly get familiar. Programs like QuarkXpress and Adobe InDesign are far more powerful and versatile… but also several times more expensive than the Microsoft Office, and a lot less easy to use. For most DTP work, PowerPoint will do everything you need.

THE BIG PICTURE   ☐ ⊟ ☒

Finally, for DTP, you will not be needing the Slide Outline nor the Slide Notes, so to get the most from the slide's view pane switch to Slide View from the View icons towards the bottom left of your PowerPoint work window.

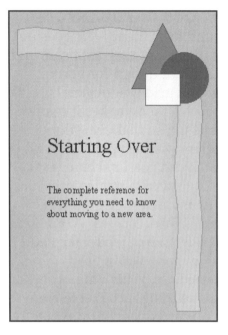

Starting Over

The complete reference for
everything you need to know
about moving to a new area.

DTP DESIGN TIPS

The design and layout of documents is an art rather than a science, and there are as many styles as there are people, but there are some guidelines that you can bear in mind to help make sure that the DTP work you do looks attractive and gets your message across clearly.

1. REMEMBER YOUR PRINTER

One basic tip is to keep in mind at all times the printer that you are going to be producing your finished document on. Different printers have different characteristics. Most common ink-jets give a slightly fuzzy finish, and colour is speckly at best, so close, thin bands of different colours might be ineffective. If you're going to print on a laser printer, you'll need to allow about 0.25 of an inch margin of blank space around the edges, because the printer can't print there, and you'll need to make sure colours have different brightnesses, as they'll look very similar otherwise in black and white.

14. "Oil".

A very double take on the standards and preconceptions of modern life, this canvas challenges us to
define the meaning in our own lives, while retaining a sense of playful irony.

£14,000

2. USE SPACE

Don't be scared to leave areas of blank space. Allowing empty areas can be a very effective style of design, one that produces an attractive, modern appearance. If you need to convey a lot of information you may not have this luxury.

This is one of the default fonts that comes with Microsoft products. It is attractive, well-balanced and easily legible.

This is a shareware font. Its letters are somewhat scraggy and too samey, and it is not easy for the reader to decipher.

A Page Title Lends A Feel Of Importance

Arranging text in columns can be rather time-consuming in Power Point, but it is often worth the effort.

SUB-TITLES ACROSS A COLUMN BREAK A PAGE UP

The bulk of your page, of course, should be made up of body text. You can put a keyline between columns if you want to, although it is not strictly necessary. The bulk of your page, of course, should be made up of body text

You can put a keyline between columns if you want to, although it is not strictly necessary. The bulk of your page, of course, should be made up of body text. You can put a keyline between columns if you want to, although it is not always going to be necessary.

The bulk of your page, of course, should be made up of body text. You can put a keyline between columns if. The bulk of your page, of course, should be made up of body text. You can put a keyline between columns. The bulk of your page, of course, should be made up of body text The bulk of your page, of course.

The bulk of your page, of course, should be made up of body text. You can put a keyline between columns if you want to, although it is not strictly necessary. The bulk of your page, of course, should be made up of body text.

You can put a keyline between columns if you want to, although it is not strictly necessary The bulk of your page, of course, should be made up of body text. You can put a keyline between columns if you want to, although it is not always going to be necessary

You can put a keyline between columns if you want to, although it is not strictly necessary The bulk of your page, of course, should be made up of body text. You can put a keyline between columns if you want to, although it is not always going to be necessary

The bulk of your page, of course, should be made up of body text. You can put a keyline between columns if. The bulk of your page, of course, should be made up of body text. You can put a keyline between columns. You can put a keyline between columns if you want to, although. The bulk of your page, of course, should be made up of body text The bulk of your page, of course, should be made up of body text

3. CHOOSE FONTS CAREFULLY

Take time selecting the font or fonts you're going to use. Although many fonts look broadly similar, they all vary in terms of the way that their individual letters appear – how thick they are, how close together they fall, even how well-drawn they are. In general, the fonts that come with Windows and Office are going to be superior in terms of weighting and balance than the shareware fonts you can get from the net or from cheap CD-ROMs. As we discussed earlier, you should avoid using too many different fonts in one document. Two or three is plenty.

4. USE VARIED DESIGN ELEMENTS

If you want to produce a professional-looking document, remember to make use of the page elements that are less obvious at a first glance – headers and footers to convey document information, such as title and page number, splitting text into separate boxes to act as columns, or stretching a title across multiple columns of lesser text. One effective technique is to use a Sans Serif font such as Tahoma for titles and a Serif font such as Times New Roman for body text.

WORKING TOGETHER

The latest version of Microsoft Office comes with a very wide range of inbuilt support programs and routines to help with internet and on-line functionality. You can use PowerPoint over the net to host your Slide Shows online, have multiple people work on a document over the net or an office network, publish PowerPoint presentations to the web as web pages and more.

MICROSOFT OFFICE SERVER EXTENSIONS

The Office Server Extensions are a range of special enhancements to the Office 2000, Internet Explorer and Windows Explorer programs that increase the capabilities of the system to link PowerPoint and other Office programs together over the internet. They help provide special functions for online publishing, group collaboration and other document management issues. Before you can use these advanced functions you will need to find a web server that has been enhanced with the Server Extensions and that allows you and the people you want to work with to access it. This is an extremely advanced operation – most of the server-side functions are quite advanced, in fact – and you should contact your IT support for further information.

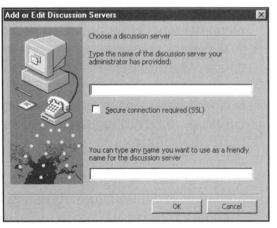

ONLINE PRESENTATIONS

You can display a presentation over the web or an intranet using the Broadcast functions. This can include standard embedded video clips and live audio narration performed via a microphone plugged into your computer's sound card. Broadcast presentations are a great way of reaching a geographically diverse audience, and all that you need to view the presentation is a standard modern web browser. The presentation is saved in a web-readable format, so that it can be viewed the same way at a later date. If you're expecting a large audience to see the presentation, or you want to send video, Microsoft recommend using a separate commercial product of theirs called NetShow to perform the broadcast.

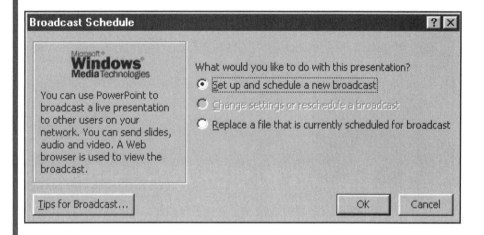

There isn't room in this book to go into all the details of setting up and running a Broadcast slideshow. You can prepare a presentation for an online broadcast by selecting Set Up and Schedule from the Online Broadcast submenu of the SLIDE SHOW menu. From the Broadcast Schedule dialog box that appears, you can view tips on setting up and running a broadcast, and you can select the Set up and schedule a new broadcast radio button, then click OK to start the set-up procedure. You'll need to specify a shared location in the server options in the Schedule a New Broadcast dialog box. Your IT support will be able to assist you.

RUNNING AN ONLINE MEETING WITH MICROSOFT NETMEETING

In Office 2000, Microsoft NetMeeting has been fully integrated into PowerPoint and the other programs. A set of functions to permit online working are included, and can run effectively integrated into the background. This special integration means that you can swap information and share discussions with people at different physical locations in real time, just as if you were all in the same office. All participants need to have Microsoft NetMeeting installed, naturally. You can access Microsoft NetMeeting and start a discussion via the Online Collaboration submenu of the TOOLS menu.

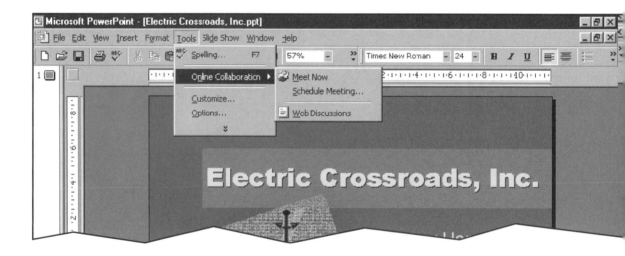

The Online Collaboration submenu lets you start an immediate NetMeeting, inviting participants to join in. NetMeeting runs in the background, sharing your file with other participants for you. As soon as one other person accepts the invitation, the meeting can begin. Microsoft NetMeeting requires that the people you involve be part of your wide-area computer network (WAN), which can be configured to include the internet but is more commonly restricted to a company intranet. Setting up a NetMeeting can be quite complex, and is beyond the scope of this book.

COLLABORATING ON A FILE IN NETMEETING

When you start a NetMeeting, you are the only participant who has control of the presentation. All the others can see your presentation, of course, but they cannot make any changes, or take any control of proceedings. Similarly, if you join a NetMeeting you will initially have no control over proceedings. However, the system can be set up so that other participants can take control of the presentation. This is enabled by turning on the Collaboration option, which must be done by the person who started the meeting. When this is active, the participants can take turns in controlling the presentation, to edit or demonstrate as appropriate. When the presentation is being controlled by someone else, whether you started the meeting or merely attended, you lose all control over your mouse pointer. The initials of the person controlling the show are placed next to the pointer, so that you can see who is in charge.

Collaboration can also be turned off by the person in control at that time. When this happens, control is passed back to the person who started the meeting. In addition, the Chat and Whiteboard functions of NetMeeting are enabled, so that everyone can discuss matters electronically and can demonstrate their thoughts on the board. Only the person who started the meeting needs to have a copy of the presentation – or, in fact, of PowerPoint at all. All functions will be run from the host's computer, and broadcast to the NetMeeting installations of the other participants.

A collaboration under the control of a colleague.

Electric Crossroads, Inc.

Company Handbook

NETWORKED FILES

There are going to be instances when you will want other users to be able to access the date you have prepared, or when you yourself need access to other people's information. Even small businesses often have computer networks now, and they are vital for larger companies. The chances are that you use a computer at work, and if you do, it is almost certain to be connected to a network. That means you need to understand some of the implications of network files.

The most common way of making a file available to more than one person is through a network. This means that

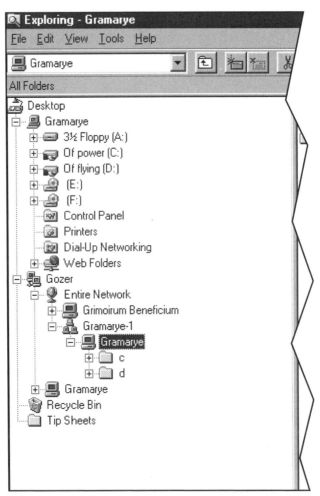

although the workbook exists on just one computer, more than one person can access it and make changes to it. Networked data may be held on a specially-dedicated network drive – usually physically located on a Network Server computer, often to be found inside an IT department – or it may be held on one user's personal machine, but with access available to other users. If you are responsible for creating a presentation that will be used and updated over a network by several people, it is well worth keeping a backup copy and regularly examining the presentation for content and errors, just in case.

BUSY FILES

If a file requires regular updating by several people – a catalogue of records, customer information list or other such presentation – then it is important not to let more than one person modify the file at a time, to avoid data loss. Almost all networks are able to change a document's readability once it is already being accessed by one person, so that if it is already in use other people will be unable to open it. Another possibility is that the file can be set to allow second and subsequent users to open a copy of the file as it was at its last save. These copies cannot usually be saved easily, so the second user will be aware that they are not able to make changes until the first user has closed down the file. Sometimes, of course, making changes won't be important – if the second user merely needs to refer to the presentation for some information, for example.

When lots of different people work on a presentation, it can get tricky to keep track of the changes. The usual convention is for each person to add a Comment to the title slide when they work on the file, explaining what they have done and when. Each time the person updates the file, their latest note should be placed on top of their previous one, not making contact with anyone else's notes. That way, the most recent modification for

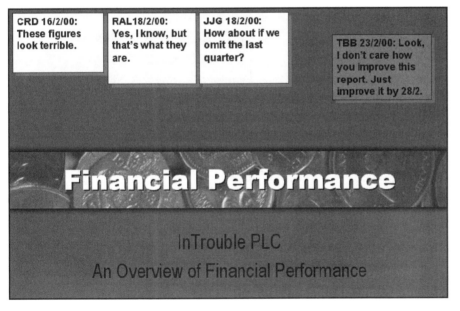

each user remains visible and date-stamped, so that it is easy to tell how recently a certain person altered a file as well as who did so most recently.

SAVING A PRESENTATION OVER THE INTERNET

FTP – short for File Transfer Protocol – is an internet tool for transferring files between computers that may be anywhere around the world. PowerPoint allows you to treat specific FTP-able locations (called FTP Sites) as another part of your hard drive or network. This lets you save files directly to an FTP site.

1 To save a file to FTP, you first need to tell your machine where to look. In the Save As dialog box, click on the Save in pick-list at the top of the screen to make it drop down. Select FTP Locations, and an option called Add/Modify FTP Locations will be displayed, along with a list of locations your system already knows about.

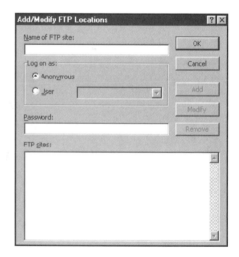

2 Either double-click the FTP site to publish to, or double-click on the Add/Modify FTP Locations option and configure the site details (check the Help system or your IT department/consultant if you are unsure how to do this). If your computer is not already linked to the internet, your computer will start your usual internet connection process.

3 Once you are connected to the FTP site, the Save As dialog box will allow you to navigate the FTP in the same way as any part of your own hard drive. Once you have located the authorized place to save your file, you may do so as normal – although backups will not be created on your system until you resave the presentation on your own computer again.

SAVING A PRESENTATION AS A WEB SITE

The basic principles of publishing a presentation as a web site – as opposed to a web-readable file, which counts as a stored broadcast – are extremely simple. Because PowerPoint Slides are treated by the program as a collection of static objects, all you have to do is choose to save your worksheet as a web page. Immediately before you do so, always save the file normally so that you can still gain access to the normal file. To get the most from it, you will want to include Action-based objects which hyperlink around your presentation in order to make navigation convenient.

1 From the <u>File</u> menu, choose the <u>Save As Web Page...</u> option.

2 The <u>Save As</u> dialog will appear. You can modify the title that the web site will be called to something other than the default file name, if you wish. Select <u>Save</u> to quickly turn the entire presentation into a web site…

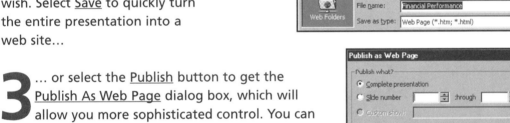

3 … or select the <u>Publish</u> button to get the <u>Publish As Web Page</u> dialog box, which will allow you more sophisticated control. You can pick a selection from your presentation, choose which browser/s to customize for and set a range of advanced options by clicking the <u>Web Options</u> box.

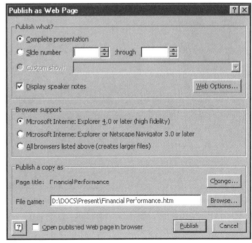

4 Click either <u>Save</u> or <u>Publish</u> (depending on which dialogue you are in), and your presentation will be turned into an HTML file or files. If multiple items are required – for example to provide support files such as external objects or pictures – then a properly-linked folder will be created along with the HTML file so that the different elements of data referred to can be accessed in a web browser. Because some elements do not necessarily appear exactly as they do on the screen, it is always worth checking your new web material by loading it into your browser before you publish it properly on the web.

There are a wide range of older program files that PowerPoint 2000 can understand. As well as being able to decipher saved presentations from all the previous versions of PowerPoint down to and including version 4.0, it can also understand web pages, text files, Harvard Graphics files, Freelance Windows files and outline files in a wide variety of formats, as well as add-ins and templates. To open an older file, select Open from the File menu, and navigate to the file as you would if it were a standard presentation. With some formats the conversion process will mean that some formatting and other advanced data gets lost, but the core information will be translated.

Saving files in a format compatible with older programs is just as easy. From the Save As... dialog off the File menu, click on the Save As type.. box, then scroll down the list until you find a type of file that is sufficient for your needs. For colleagues with older versions of PowerPoint on the PC, the best file type is generally the one called PowerPoint 97-2000 & 95 Presentation – quite a mouthful, but it is an extremely versatile format. For colleagues who will want to use your file on a Macintosh computer, the best file type to select is the one called PowerPoint 95, which is compatible with recent versions of PowerPoint for the Mac. You can also save your presentation as a number of different picture file formats (one file per slide), including CompuServe GIFs (.gif), JPEGs (.jpg), TIFFs (.tif), Metafiles (.wmf), and Bitmaps (.bmp). These are easily readable as a static picture, but next to impossible to edit or to view as a timed/animated slide show.

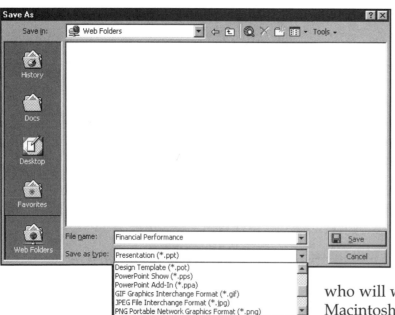

Choose the file format you wish to save in from the Save As dialog box.

REFERENCE SECTION

10

Although Microsoft Office goes out of its way to make all its programs as easy as possible, not everyone is happy with the layout and functions available. You can change around the icons and toolbars to get them exactly the way you want and you can create new sub-programs, called Macros, to make tasks you repeat often more convenient. This last chapter will cover the ways you can make your copy of PowerPoint your very own, as well as looking more closely at the different AutoContent presentations available.

Customizing Toolbars

There are a number of ways you can change the configuration of the icon toolbars that PowerPoint offers you. The toolbars themselves are a great time-saving resource, and often include options that are not quite the same as their menu item counterparts – even when, unlike the View icons, the same options are available.

RAFTING THE STANDARD AND FORMATTING TOOLBARS

If you don't always use PowerPoint in full-screen mode, having the Standard and Formatting toolbars on one line can get inconvenient, with different buttons being hidden. The buttons that would normally fall off the edge of the window are still accessible by clicking the small right-arrows at the end of the bar, but that can hold you up a bit. You can tell PowerPoint to place the toolbars on separate lines, known as rafting, to get much better access to the icons. Click on the Customize… option on the Tools menu, and select the Options tab of the Customize dialogue. Under Personalized Menus and Toolbars, deselect Standard and Formatting Toolbars share one row, and click OK. The two toolbars will be switched to separate rows, the Formatting toolbar beneath the Standard one.

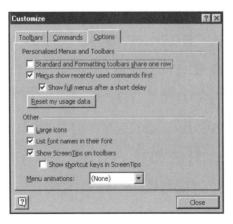

POSITIONING THE TOOLBARS

It is possible to move the toolbars around to different positions on the screen according to your needs and preferences. Each

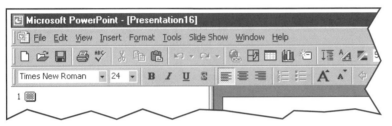

toolbar has a default position, including ones that are not automatically displayed at start-up, and it may be useful to change those positions from time to time.

Every toolbar that is part of the screen borders, including the menu bar, begins with a small line across the width of the bar. This is the handle by which you can pick up the toolbar and move it around. When the cursor runs over the line, it changes to a four-directional cross-like arrow. At this point, you can click and hold the mouse button to drag the toolbar around the screen. Toolbars can switch between three different mode: a horizontal bar (the default for the major bars) which is activated by moving the bar to the top or bottom edge of the

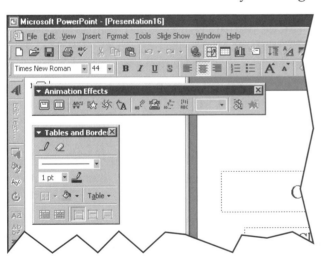

window; a vertical bar, which is activated when you move a bar on to the left-hand edge of the window; and a floating palette, activated by moving the bar away from the edges. In addition, floating palettes can be resized through a number of standard sizes by clicking on the edges and resizing them as you would a window.

If you aren't happy with the effect you achieve, you can move the toolbar back to its old position easily.

REMEMBER

You can display or hide a toolbar by respectively selecting or deselecting it from the list that appear when you highlight Toolbars from the VIEW menu.

ADDING AND MOVING BUTTONS

In addition to changing the range of different toolbars accessible to you and their positions on the screen, you can also modify which buttons appear within a specific toolbar. From the <u>Customize</u> dialog box, make sure the <u>Commands</u> tab is selected.

To remove a button from a toolbar, click on the button and keep the mouse held (the button will be surrounded by a black box), then drag the button off the toolbar. A small cross will appear in the box, and if you let go of the mouse, the button will be deleted. To move a button to a new location (including on a new toolbar), click on it and drag it to its new location. The insertion point will be indicated by a black insertion mark at the point the button will move to. Buttons cannot be placed on top of each other. Marking a button as <u>Begin a Group</u> (from the right-click pop-up menu) puts a small grey bar in front of the button.

ADD AND REMOVE BUTTONS

You can also add and remove a selection of pre-defined icons from the toolbars by clicking the <u>Add or Remove Buttons</u> option from the down-icon at the end of each toolbar. Select this, and a list of buttons that Microsoft think the toolbar is normally associated with will appear; you can deselect an item to get rid of it, or select it to add it. This is a lot less flexible than the method above, though.

CREATING A NEW BUTTON

To add a button, you need to select the appropriate command from the <u>Command</u> tab of the <u>Customize</u> dialogue box. Click on the list of menu titles in the left-hand list, and all the commands that fall under that category will be displayed in the right-hand list by name and icon. Macro commands that you have created will be displayed under the <u>Macros</u> heading. Click and drag the command you wish to use on to the appropriate menu bar, which will expand (as much as possible) to accommodate it. If the command has an icon, that will be displayed as the new button; otherwise the name will be displayed.

Once in place, however, a button image can be modified. Click on the button you wish to change, and then click the <u>Modify Selection</u> button. The <u>Modify</u> menu will appear. Click on the <u>Change Button Image</u> selection, and a small palette of icon options will be shown to you.

Edit the icons you assign to a toolbar with the Modify Selection popup menu.

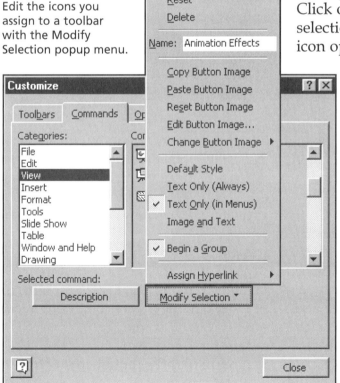

You may select one for the button you are modifying. Alternatively, you can click on the <u>Edit Button Image</u> selection to call up the <u>Button Editor</u>. Click on a colour and then on a square in the large-scale image to change a pixel in the 16x16 grid. The <u>Erase</u> character is shown as transparent in the final button. When you are happy with the finished icon, click <u>OK</u>, and your custom icon image will be applied.

AUTOCONTENT TEMPLATES

The next few pages will list the specifics of the different templates, discussing what you would use each one for, what information you would need to complete them, and their strengths and weaknesses.

THE PRESENTATIONS

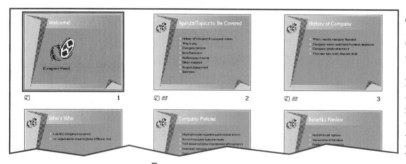

Title: Employee Orientation.
Category: Corporate.
Uses: Passing key information about company policy & history to new staff.
Info Needed: Principal personnel, staff benefits, which forms need to be filled in, company policy, vision and history.
Strengths + Limitations: Allows you to bring all your key information for new staff together into one place, but non-standard information will mean you have to rewrite some slides.

Title: Company Meeting.
Category: Corporate.
Uses: Annual presentation describing company performance over the last year, and goals for the year to come.
Info Needed: Financial data for the last 12 months, a record of targets and whether or not they were met, info on current staffing levels, outgoings and so on.
Strengths + Limitations: Good overview of the year with a discussion of the next 12 months, but elements may be irrelevant for smaller companies.

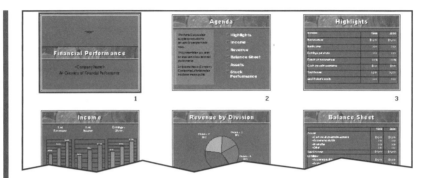

Title: Financial Overview.
Category: Corporate.
Uses: Presenting data on financial performance to third parties.
Info Needed: Detailed accounts and sales figures.
Strengths + Limitations: Provides a great framework for arranging your financial data for display, but is really best suited to a larger company.

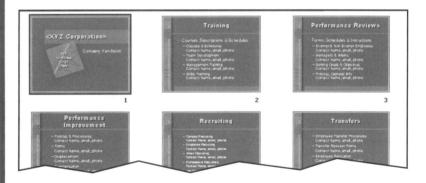

Title: Company Handbook.
Category: Corporate.
Uses: Providing staff with a complete list of who to contact in every eventuality.
Info Needed: Names, email addresses and phone numbers of all staff responsible for all personnel functions.
Strengths + Limitations: You end up with a superb database of contact information, but it needs to be kept carefully up to date.

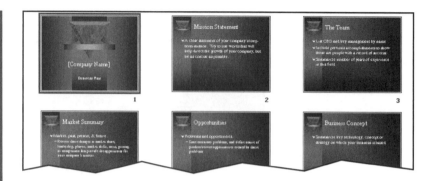

Title: Business Plan.
Category: Corporate.
Uses: Presenting an overview of a business idea in order to secure funding.
Info Needed: The business concept, competitors, your marketing plan, how the business will generate profits, and projected account balances and other financial figures for the first three years.
Strengths + Limitations: A good, well-balanced business plan, but perhaps a bit too short. Many business plans are 50–60 pages or more.

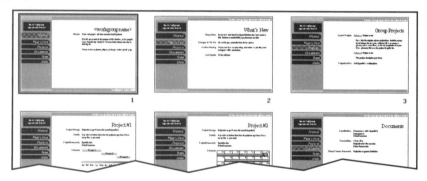

Title: Group Home Page.
Category: Corporate.
Uses: Establishing a presence on the web that introduces a small company or project team.
Info Needed: Personnel details, projects being worked on, team members' interests.
Strengths + Limitations: Gives a quick and easy framework for creating a web site, but the contents are quite brief and limited.

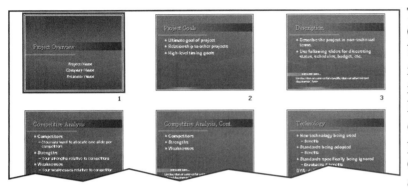

Title: Project Overview
Category: Projects.
Uses: To detail a project, from implementation to financial targets.
Info Needed: Project details, including strategic plans, financial expectations, key personnel and so on.
Strengths + Limitations: Acts as a good mnemonic aid to preparing all the requisite information, but companies large enough to require project overviews will generally have a pre-defined house style that you have to follow.

Title: Reporting Progress or Status.
Category: Projects.
Uses: A follow-up to the Project Overview, used to detail the progress of a project and whether or not it is meeting targets.
Info Needed: Schedules, goals and expectations in place when the project was started, and how real life matches up to them.
Strengths + Limitations: Allows for a detailed discussion of a project, but does rather expect that the scope of the work falls within fairly narrow lines. Some rewriting may be necessary.

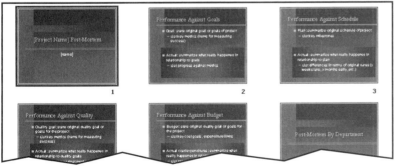

Title: Project Post-Mortem.
Category: Projects.
Uses: To hold a debrief once a project has been completed.
Info Needed: Initial goals, schedules and budgets and final performance, timing and accounts.
Strengths + Limitations: This is a detailed analysis, allowing for a lot of cross-comparison to demonstrate a wide range of different aspects fully.

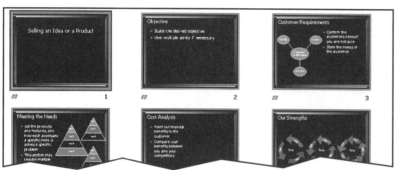

Title: Selling a Product or Service.
Category: Sales.
Uses: Providing data about a product so as to persuade others to purchase it.
Info Needed: Product details and specifications, information on competitors and why your product is better, some idea of the potential customers' needs and budgets.
Strengths + Limitations: A solid, hard-hitting sales pitch, but might be too aggressive for some clients.

Title: Product/Services Overview.
Category: Sales.
Uses: Providing data about a product so that others can decide whether they want to purchase it or not.
Info Needed: Product details, specifications and areas of excellence, along with some financial data
Strengths + Limitations: A good framework for passing out detailed information on a product, but might be a bit weak to convince clients who need to be closed.

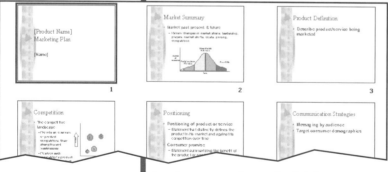

Title: Marketing Plan.
Category: Sales.
Uses: To detail the marketing and advertising strategy for a product or service.
Info Needed: Marketing strategy details, expected cross-market exposure, budgets, projected yield.
Strengths + Limitations: Very solid for traditional marketing strategies, but doesn't necessarily take the full range of modern cutting-edge marketing opportunities into account, particularly in new media.

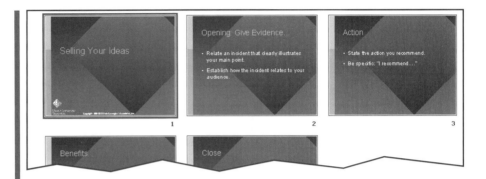

Title: Selling Your Ideas.
Category: Carnegie Coach.
Uses: Presenting recommendations or policy suggestions in a persuasive manner.
Info Needed: An real-life example of how your suggestion can help, specific action points to be taken and detailed commentary on how these will aid the situation.
Strengths + Limitations: Provides an effective, sales-led framework for putting your view across.

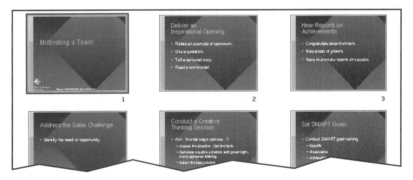

Title: Motivating a Team.
Category: Carnegie Coach.
Uses: Getting a team of people enthusiastic and motivated to work together.
Info Needed: Positive achievements (and the related people) to focus on, a positive view of the current challenge, measurable goals to focus on.
Strengths + Limitations: An extensive and well-balanced motivational tool.

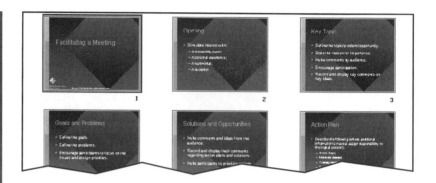

Title: Facilitating a Meeting.
Category: Carnegie Coach.
Uses: A generic template to allow you to structure
a meeting effectively.
Info Needed: Meeting goals and problems, strengths and
weaknesses of the participants.
Strengths + Limitations: A positive, solid meeting structure,
although somewhat too generic and simplified for many
purposes.

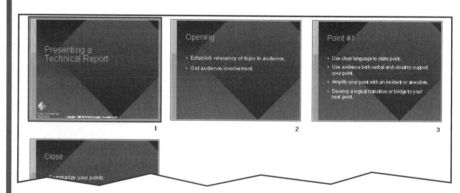

Title: Presenting a Technical Report.
Category: Carnegie Coach.
Uses: To help a technical specialist convey important
information to a non-technical audience.
Info Needed: A good understanding of the audience, and the
issues that they will consider relevant.
Strengths + Limitations: Provides a faultless structure, but is
perhaps a bit terse.

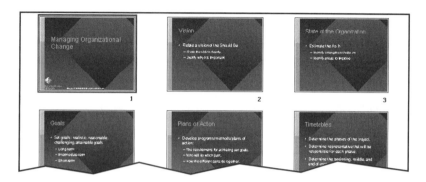

Title: Managing Organizational Change.
Category: Carnegie Coach.
Uses: To help reassure and inform staff during a period of restructuring.
Info Needed: A clear picture of the current situation and the end result, along with the costs involved, both financial and actual.
Strengths + Limitations: Detailed and informative, but you may need to reassure staff clearly and precisely about job changes to avoid concern.

Title: Introducing and Thanking a Speaker.
Category: Carnegie Coach.
Uses: To provide a framework for a guest speaker's speech.
Info Needed: Details about the speaker and their relevance.
Strengths + Limitations: Effective and to the point, but does not actually tell you much more than the title itself does, as it involves just one slide.

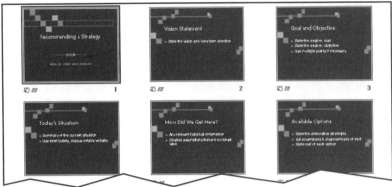

Title: Recommending a Strategy.
Category: General.
Uses: Analysing a situation and suggesting a reaction to it.
Info Needed: Details of the current situation, historical information leading to it, different possible responses and explanations of why your answer is superior to the others.
Strengths + Limitations: Comprehensive and effective, with plenty of allowance for non-standard issues.

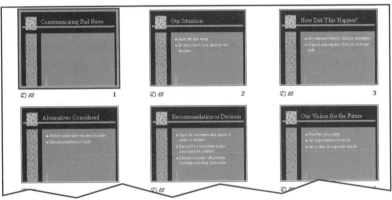

Title: Communicating Bad News.
Category: General.
Uses: To clearly state what has happened when something goes wrong, and how to move forward.
Info Needed: A precise and accurate picture of the current situation, along with a solid, approved strategy for turning the situation around.
Strengths + Limitations: Giving bad news is always difficult, but this presentation makes it as bearable as possible. More suited to a subordinate audience than a superior one.

Title: Brainstorming Session.
Category: General.
Uses: To chair a meeting that needs to generate ideas.
Info Needed: The topic concerned.
Strengths + Limitations: The material is good, but results will depend on the creativity of the participants, and there is no way around that.

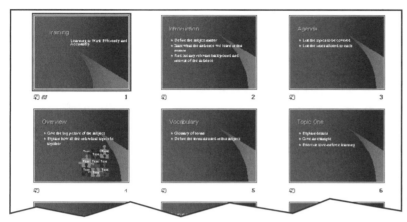

Title: Training.
Category: General.
Uses: A meeting where you will be teaching people or passing on knowledge.
Info Needed: A good understanding of the material you are teaching, and a progression of the information in topics from basic to advanced.
Strengths + Limitations: *A good, general structure, but may need tailoring to fit the specific type of training being carried out.*

Title: Certificate.
Category: General.
Uses: To reward a staff member with a certificate of excellence.
Info Needed: The recipient's name, and what they have achieved.
Strengths + Limitations: It's not a presentation, just a blank form.

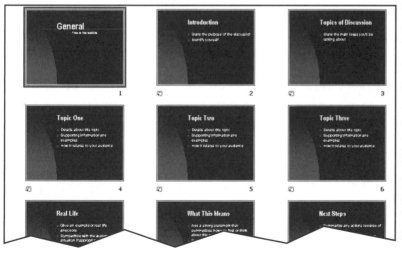

Title: Generic.
Category: General.
Uses: A general meeting template when nothing else seems suitable.
Info Needed: The purpose of the meeting, and what you want to say in it.
Strengths + Limitations: A good, general meeting structure. It will need to be tailored to fit your specific needs, however.

WORKING WITH MACROS

In this section you'll learn how to use macros to automate a wide range of tasks within PowerPoint. If you carry out any sort of repetitive activity, macros can easily save you the bother of carrying out exactly the same sequences of keystrokes, mouse movements and/or menu selections over and over again.

WHAT IS A MACRO?

A macro is a small program within PowerPoint, which, when activated, affects a presentation. Don't worry if you don't know how to write programs, though: PowerPoint can be told to "record" a sequence of events as you carry them out – opening a menu, selecting an item, clicking on a button and so on – and turn that recording into a macro. The macro produced can then be added as a Custom toolbar button, given a special key shortcut or opened in the Macro Editor and altered or enhanced.

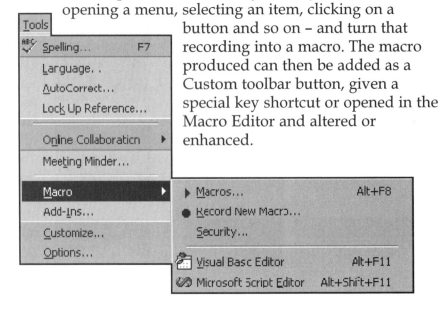

The Macro sub menu provides access to the macro editing and recording functions.

WHAT SORTS OF THINGS CAN MACROS DO?

"Recorded" macros can mimic any user activity that takes place while the <u>Macro Record</u> facility is switched on. For instance, a macro could record the user selecting and deleting a placeholder, applying a new slide layout and then placing a shadowed box in the background. Whenever that particular macro was run, the same set of instructions and actions would automatically be carried out, in the same as they were initially recorded.

Macros can also record and playback dialog boxes being opened, receiving data, and being closed, running slideshows or even swapping between different presentations. You can record loading and saving files, importing material, moving boxes around a slide and much more.

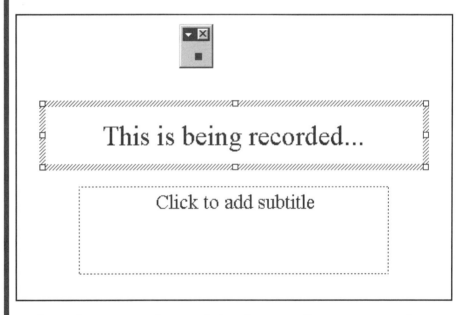

In fact, if you move beyond simply recording macros and write macros directly into the Macro Editor you can get a macro to do almost anything, including the most complex calculations and data manipulation. This is extremely complex, however, and unless you know your way around Visual Basic and the Microsoft VB Applications Development Environment, you'd be well advised not to try.

RECORDING A MACRO

Recording a macro is simple, but you must plan what you want to record before starting the Macro Recorder – if you make a mistake while recording a macro, that mistake will be recorded as well, so a little thought can save you some problems. Select the Macro item from the Tools menu, and click on Record New Macro. A dialog box will appear, allowing you to name your macro and decide where to store it. It is probably best to leave the Macro name and Store macro in options as their defaults – changing the name or location can cause certain bugs to arise. You can also add a description of the macro here in the Description box for later reference, and it is best to do so, so that you know what the various macros are.

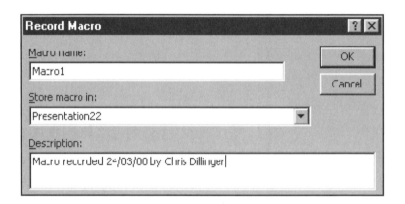

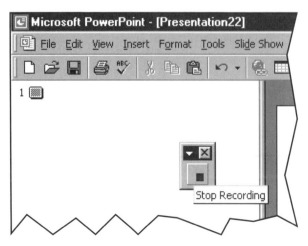

From the moment you click OK, the Macro Recorder will be working, so make sure you know exactly what you want to record.

When you click OK, a floating toolbar will appear. Now carry out whatever PowerPoint activity you want to record and when you've finished, click the small blue square Stop Recording box in the floating toolbar, which ends recording.

THE MACRO DIALOG BOX

The <u>Macro</u> dialog box is accessed from the <u>Macros…</u> item on the <u>Macro</u> submenu of the <u>Tools</u> menu. It is from here that you can run macros, edit or delete them or alter the macro options.

To run a macro that you have previously recorded, highlight its name in the <u>Macro</u> dialog box and click <u>Run</u> (or double-click on the name). The macro will run and the Macro Dialogue Box will disappear. <u>Step Into</u> and <u>Edit</u> will both open the <u>Visual Basic for Applications Development Environment</u>, where you can actually write the code for a macro directly. <u>Step Into</u> will run the first command in the macro and is used for debugging a macro that isn't working as it is supposed to, while <u>Edit</u> just brings up the macro code for you to tinker with.

If you enter a name in the <u>Macro Name</u> text entry box that doesn't correspond to a macro, you can then click on <u>Create</u>, which will start the <u>Visual Basic for Applications Development Environment</u>, allowing you to write a new macro from scratch. Clicking on <u>Delete</u> when a macro name is highlighted will delete that macro.

GLOSSARY

Translation is a difficult process, but all it takes is practice. Here are a few key words an phrases that you may have missed during the course of this book.

ACTION
A function or command activated by clicking on or moving the mouse over a Drawing Object.

ANIMATION
Making graphical elements move in real-time, specifically (in PowerPoint) with respect to objects on a Slide in a Slide Show. Animations between Slides are called Transitions.

AUTOCONTENT
The selection of pre-written Presentations provided by Microsoft that provide a template for your own work.

AUTOCORRECT
The Microsoft Office facility that lets PowerPoint correct your spelling for you automatically.

AUTOLAYOUT
One of 24 pre-defined Slide layout templates.

AUTOSHAPE
An outline with a pre-defined shape that can be scaled and otherwise modified.

BULLET
The small symbol at the beginning of each item in a list of items.

BUTTON
Another word for Icon.

CHART
A Graph or other visual representation of data.

CLIP ART
A small, free piece of simple artwork.

COMMENT
A note that can be added to a Slide without disturbing its contents.

DOCUMENT
A File that stores one set of data created by and modifiable by a program.

DRAWING OBJECT
An individual item on a Slide.

FILE
A set of data on a computer's disk drive(s) that makes up one complete, functioning, discrete item.

FOOTER
The information that appears at the bottom of every page in a Document.

GRAPH
A visual representation of different items of data used for comparison.

HEADER
The information that appears at the top of every page in a Document.

ICON
A small graphical image that functions as a short-cut to a command or option when you click on it.

MACRO
A user-defined program, function, command or recording of activity that can be repeated by the user.

MASTER
A template that provides a background for each Slide, and also defines default text styles, slide colour schemes and the position of Placeholders.

MEDIA CLIP
A Document that changes or displays in real-time; a Movie, animation or Sound File.

MENU
A box of vertically-aligned commands or options that appears when you click on its title.

MOVIE
A Document that holds a short film that you can watch.

NARRATION
The process of recording Sound Files of a speech, Slide by slide, to accompany a Slide Show.

OBJECT
A document created by another program imported into PowerPoint that can be edited from within it by calling up the creating program, and which will update itself within the Presentation as the original file is updated. In effect, a window onto another Document file.

ORGANIZATION CHART
A visual representation of the power structure within an organisation.

PATTERN
A pre-set arrangement of lines and/or dots, generally coloured.

PICTURE
A Document containing a static visual image.

PLACEHOLDER
A box that appears on a Slide while it is being edited to indicate where certain types of information should go.

PRESENTATION
An entire PowerPoint Document. Presentations can of course be as short as just one Slide.

SLIDE SHOW
An automatic function that displays the Slides in a Presentation on the computer screen one after another.

SLIDE
One page of a PowerPoint Document.

SOUND FILE
A Document that holds a sound that you can listen to.

TABLE
A collection of straight lines that divide an area into individual cells.

TEXTURE
A Picture that can be repeated next to itself without showing visible seams.

TIMING
The pre-set pause between Animation on a Slide, and between slides themselves, during a Slide Show.

TOOLBAR
A collection of Icon short-cuts to commands or options that usually share a common theme or area of effect.

TOOL-TIP
The word or phrase describing an Icon's purpose that appears when you hold your mouse pointer still over it for a second or so.

TRANSITION
A graphical animation of the process of changing from one Slide to another during a Slide Show.

WIZARD
A sub-program within PowerPoint that automates certain areas of a task for you or otherwise provides you with help or makes working faster and easier.

WORDART
Microsoft Office's special program for applying graphical filters to a word or phrase.

WEB ADDRESSES

RESOURCES
The first place to look for additional information is of course the Microsoft homepage, found at http://www.microsoft.com. This site is huge, but there is a very efficient search facility throughout and help, as for all Microsoft products, is available at the click of a button. It helps to know exactly what you need before going there though.

UPDATES AND PRODUCT FIXES
http://www.microsoft.com/downloads

FONTS
Try one of the following for free fonts:
http://www.microsoft.com/typography/fontpack
http://www.fontfree.com

LANGUAGE ADD-ONS
http://msdn.microsoft.com/officedev/downloads/

ENTERPRISE SUPPORT
http://www.microsoft.com/office/enterprise/entsupport.htm

CLIPART
In one of your favourite search engines, type "free clipart". You will see that there are lots of sites dedicated to providing

you with free stuff. Most of these sites are private and all of them are crammed with freebies, usually arranged by easy to browse categories. http://www.clipartconnection.com is one of them, along with http://www.artclipart.com. All these sites have links to other freebies sites, so don't hesitate to have a look around for that special piece of clip art. Clip art is usually copyright free, but do make sure before you use it.

http://www.clipartconnection.com
http://www.artclipart.com
http://officeupdate.microsoft.com/2000/downloadDetails/

TEMPLATES
Sample Templates:
http://officeupdate.microsoft.com/2000/downloadDetails/Template.htm

MACROS
http://officeupdate.microsoft.com/2000/
http://www.mindspring.com/~tflynn/excelvba.html
http://www.evirus.com

HELP
http://support.microsoft.com/support/
http://msdn.microsoft.com/resources/
http://officeupdate.microsoft.com/welcome/
http://officeupdate.microsoft.com/2000/articlelist/
http://officeupdate.microsoft.com/articlelist/
http://support.microsoft.com
http://www.microsoft.com/downloads/

INDEX